The Power of Positive Self-Discipline

7 Easy Techniques to Strengthen
Willpower, Enhance Mental Toughness,
and (Confidently) Reach Your Goals
Without Struggle

Logan Mind

Copyright © 2024 - All rights reserved.

EMOTIONAL INTELLIGENCE

for Social Success

FREE DOWNLOAD: pxl.to/loganmindfreebook

LOGAN MIND

EXTRAS

Get Your FREE Book!

As a way of saying thanks for your purchase, I'm offering the book **Emotional Intelligence for Social Success** absolutely **FREE** to my readers.

Inside the book, you will find:

- Techniques to master self-awareness and control your emotions
- Strategies to improve your social skills and forge meaningful relationships
- Tips on handling conflicts gracefully and constructively
- Ways to boost your empathy for better personal and professional connections
- Methods for enhancing your communication skills

If you want to elevate your emotional intelligence and excel in your social interactions, make sure to grab this free book.

How to get the book:

- Follow the below link
- Click on **FREE Book**
- Insert the language
- Download Your Book!

To get instant access just go to:

https://pxl.to/LoganMind

How to Download Your Extras

You're about to **start** a transformative path toward achieving your goals with self-discipline. To support you in maximizing the value you gain from this book, I've created some **valuable extras**. These tools are not just add-ons but pivotal resources that can help you reinforce and apply the techniques you'll learn.

Let's meet the extras:

- **Extra 1:** A **practical PDF 21-Day Challenge** tailored to the techniques discussed in the book. This step-by-step guide will facilitate your journey in developing new habits and willpower over 21 days - Worth 14.99$.
- **Extra 2:** Audio tips from experts on mastering self-discipline and mental toughness in everyday scenarios. Perfect for those who prefer listening on the go.
- **Extra 3:** A motivational playlist to keep you inspired and focused while you work towards your goals - worth 9.99$.
- **Bonus: Emotional Intelligence for Social Success** - A comprehensive guide to understanding and developing your emotional intelligence to improve interpersonal relationships, crucial for achieving broader life goals - worth 14.99$.

To access these powerful resources, here's what you need to do:

- **Follow the below link**
- **Click on the book cover**
- **Click on EXTRAS**

- **Insert the language you speak**
- **Click Download**
- **Download from the page that opens up afterwards**

Check out the extras here:

https://pxl.to/LoganMind

Interested in Other Topics?

While the methods you discover in this book are crucial, broadening your scope with related subjects can significantly amplify your growth. Each technique and principle stands stronger when complemented by other elements essential for self-mastery.

- **Building a Positive Mindset:** Enhancing your self-discipline is incredible, but a well-rounded success also requires a **positive mindset**. My book, "The Art of Positive Thinking," lays out practical strategies to train your mind towards positivity. This, in turn, creates a fertile ground for your self-discipline efforts to flourish.

- **Mastering Daily Routines:** Discipline thrives with good habits. For a deeper look into creating meaningful routines, don't miss "Daily Rituals for Peak Performance." This guides you step-by-step through crafting daily habits that optimize your time and energy, working seamlessly with what you glean from this book.

- **Mental Resilience Techniques:** Mental toughness isn't solely willpower; it's also about **resilience**. My upcoming release, "How to Build Unbreakable Mental Resilience," delves into techniques to weather life's storms. Resilience ensures that your newfound discipline is resilient to setbacks and challenges.

Each of these books offers integral pieces to the mastery puzzle. You can elevate your growth beyond what's in these pages, creating a holistic approach tailored to you.

Here's how to find the books:

- **Follow the below link**
- **Click on All My Books**
- **Grab the ones that interest you**
- **In case you want to get in touch with me, you can find all the contacts at the end of the below link.**

Check out the books and contacts here:

https://pxl.to/LoganMind

Join my Review Team!

Thank you so much for reading my book! Your support means the world to me. Your feedback is invaluable, and I would love to invite you to join my **Review Team**. As an avid reader, you have an opportunity to get a free copy of my book in exchange for your honest feedback. This would be incredibly helpful to ensure continued quality.

Joining the **ARC team** is simple! Just follow these steps:

- Click on the link or scan the QR code.
- Click on the book cover in the page that opens up.
- Click on "Join Review Team."
- Sign Up to BookSprout.
- Get notified every time I release a new book.

Check out the extras here:

https://pxl.to/LoganMind

Introduction

"You have power over your mind—not outside events. Realize this, and you will find strength." – Marcus Aurelius

Have you ever felt like your goals are just **beyond reach**, slipping through your fingers no matter how hard you try? Maybe you set out with the best intentions, only to find yourself falling back into old habits or getting distracted by life's countless twists and turns. Don't worry, we've all been there. And that's where this book steps in, offering a practical, accessible guide to transform those frustrating experiences into **genuine success**.

Self-discipline—not exactly the most glamorous word in today's instant-gratification world, is it? How many times have we blamed lack of motivation or external circumstances for our setbacks? But here's the twist: self-discipline doesn't have to be a grueling slog. It can actually be a **positive force** in your life, full of empowering moments that help you become your best self...all without constant struggle.

Why listen to what I have to say? Well, over the years, I've spent time dissecting the mechanics of human behavior, talking with some of the brightest minds, and experiencing my own myriad challenges and victories. I've penned several books exploring the nuances of psychology, philosophy, and communication. And much of this foundation has laid the groundwork for my consultancy and coaching gigs. It's a fascinating thing—to watch people transform right before your eyes, simply by applying a few fundamental techniques and shifting the way they think.

In this book, we'll **explore** the very building blocks of self-discipline, rooted in relatable scientific principles and peppered with psychological insights. You'll see how emotions play a role and understand the inner workings of the brain when it comes to willpower. Have you heard about the Marshmallow Test—the one where kids were given a choice between one marshmallow right now or two marshmallows if they waited? Well, such studies are a treasure trove for practical lessons in self-discipline.

Mindset shifts? We've got those too. You'll learn to **overcome fear and status quo bias**, tools that have historically kept us in our comfort zones. Resilience isn't just for leaders or military individuals; it's for you and me—ordinary people trying to better themselves and their lives.

Then, there's the whole topic of **mental toughness.** Actually, what does it mean to be mentally tough? It's about focus, concentration, and most importantly, impulse control. Sometimes, it's learning to say "no" to yourself—to delay gratification. Guess what? Your brain can be trained, just like a muscle, to improve these facets of self-discipline.

In your pursuit of success, goal setting is pivotal. Are you familiar with setting SMART goals?? These are goals that are Specific, Measurable, Achievable, Relevant, and Time-bound. Trust me, smashing those goals feels exhilarating. And there are visualization techniques that'll steer you clearly toward what you're striving for.

And hey, ever noticed that forming new habits is way harder than you thought it would be? Morning routines that go beyond hitting the Snooze button, techniques like habit stacking, and even something as powerful as a simple diet—these are the specifics we'll **dive into** to streamline your path.

Yet with any endeavor, there are pitfalls. How many times have procrastination or unrealistic expectations thrown us off our path? Strategies like the "40% Rule" can radically change the way you persist through challenging times.

From there, let's explore practical techniques for boosting time management. If you've worked through the Pomodoro Technique or know the Eisenhower Matrix, fantastic! You'll discover how to incorporate these into your day efficiently. For those unfamiliar, you'll soon wonder how you ever managed to get anything done without them.

Consistency may *seem* mundane, but it's the linchpin of lasting change. If you can make positive discipline a part of your life, the effects can extend into every nook and cranny of what you do. Sustaining that drive over the long haul isn't just a concept; it's doable. With methods explored in this book, lasting results are well within reach.

So, grab whatever personal development tools you favor and get comfy. We're about to enrich our lives with lessons that have scientific teeth and practical claws. Next, we will establish just how integral these continued efforts are for perpetual improvement. You don't have to walk this path alone. We're in this together.

Ready? Let's crack open the secrets behind self-discipline and start transforming challenges into opportunities. The power has always been inside you; we just need to tap into it in a structured, positive, and confident way.

Part 1: Laying the Foundation

Chapter 1: The Science of Positive Discipline

"Between stimulus and response, there is a space. In that space lies our freedom and power to choose our response."

Welcome to the intriguing world of **Positive Discipline** — more than just a tool for teaching or correcting behavior, it's a gateway to lifelong learning and self-control. In this chapter, we'll explore the magic behind it, delving into the *scientific underpinnings* that make Positive Discipline work so well.

Ever wondered why some people seem to stay calm in the trickiest situations while others just can't? Well, it's not about magic or luck — it's about **understanding** the *biological basis* of *self-control*. Our brains are wired in fascinating ways to manage willpower and emotions, which play a huge role in how we discipline ourselves and others.

Think about this: Imagine having the power to turn emotional chaos into calm and productive behavior. Tempting, right? This chapter promises to uncover the emotional foundations that drive self-discipline. By grasping these insights, you can achieve healthier relationships and *mental health*.

Get ready to learn, laugh, and maybe even ponder how all of these elements interconnect to benefit your daily life... Let's embark on this enlightening journey through Positive Discipline.

Keep reading to see how it all connects.

Understanding Positive Discipline

Positive discipline is like a trusty sidekick that helps guide behavior rather than punish it. It's built on the foundations of building trust and respect between people. Unlike punitive discipline, which relies on penalties and negative consequences to correct behavior, positive discipline wants to address the root issues and guide you gently to better ways of doing things. Imagine, instead of being scolded, you're supported and encouraged to find the right path yourself. It feels kinder, right? That's because it is!

Let's think about it. Positive discipline uses reinforcement through encouragement and support—a pat on the back when you get things right, or a gentle nudge to help when you're slightly off track. This approach makes it easier to stay motivated and learn from mistakes without feeling awful. It's about gently steering the ship rather than trying to control with an iron grip. Mistakes are seen as learning opportunities—chances to grow stronger and wiser, rather than failures.

Positive discipline promotes long-term behavioral change. When people are guided with kindness and encouragement, they tend to internalize the lessons deeply. It sets the stage for building habits that stick around because they make sense and feel good, rather than habits you stick to just to avoid getting in trouble.

Here's something to ponder:

"The approach of teaching with patience, understanding and persistence, often yields much more robust and lasting change than teaching with force or fear."

It's true, isn't it? For example, if a child messes up their homework, a negative approach would entail taking away their TV time or grounding them. In contrast, a positive discipline method would mean sitting with them, understanding where they struggled, and working through the problem together. It forges a connection, fosters confidence, and builds long-lasting skills.

Over time, this kind of encouragement shapes behavior. Imagine an employee who constantly misses deadlines. If all they get is a stern warning or a threat, they might shape up—but only out of fear. However, if they are offered support, like help in time management or a restructured workload, they will learn how to manage better. They won't just avoid missing deadlines out of fear; they'll understand how to meet them with confidence.

Small actions of encouragement can establish a positive cycle where success breeds more success. Here's where it gets insightful: Offering constructive feedback rather than punishment makes people willing to face their shortcomings because they don't feel attacked. Using phrases like, "I noticed you're struggling with this, how can I help?" instead of, "Why can't you get this right?" transforms the entire dynamic. ***Encouragement transforms blame into motivation.***

When uplifted for their efforts, people feel seen and valued. There's **strength** in knowing that failures aren't the end; they are steps forward. Guidance over criticism, and see how naturally growth follows.

To recap all this goodness:

- **Support and encouragement go a long way.**
- Focus on guiding rather than punishing.
- Mistakes are valuable learning opportunities.
- **Adopt an approach that nurtures and builds rather than knocks down.**

Having this perspective might just make tackling even the toughest challenges feel achievable, all while building a healthier outlook on self-discipline.

Alright, that's a good spot to pause and let it all sink in. Conversations built on understanding, patience, and help pave the way to positive discipline. Small steps, big impact—you'll see.

The Biological Basis of Self-Control

Alright, let's get into it. **Self-control** might seem like more of an abstract concept, but there's a whole lot of brain activity making it happen. Picture yourself standing in front of a cake—your mouth is watering, but you decide, "Nah, I shouldn't." That very decision, my friends, is largely thanks to a particular part of your brain called the prefrontal cortex.

The prefrontal cortex sits right behind your forehead, and it's like the brain's headquarters for planning, decision-making, and moderating social behavior. It's the part that kicks in when you're faced with that tempting slice of cake and helps you weigh the consequences—"Will I feel good after eating this, or will I regret it?" **Neuroscience tells us that the prefrontal cortex** is crucial for self-control. When it's working well, you're better at resisting temptations and making decisions that align with your long-term goals.

But hold on—there's more happening up there. **This process also involves neurotransmitters**—the brain's chemical messengers. Dopamine, for instance, tends to get a lot of attention. Sure, it's famed for making us feel pleasure ("Yes, cake is tasty!"), but it also plays a part in reward prediction. When you resist the cake, your brain's dopamine system might still be rewarding you in subtler ways, like making you feel proud for sticking to a healthy habit.

Then there's serotonin, which is often nicknamed the "well-being" neurotransmitter. It helps with mood regulation and can increase feelings of satisfaction—even when you're **saying no** to the cake.

Together, dopamine and serotonin balance each other out, influencing how you make decisions and exert self-control.

Here's a neat tidbit... Looking at self-control from an evolutionary perspective, we humans developed this trait (and thank goodness for that). Our ancestors needed it—imagine surviving in a harsh environment where you had to resist the urge to eat all your food supplies at once. Instead, they had to plan and ration, cultivating patience and foresight...critical elements in the scheme of self-preservation.

Let's put it this way: self-control isn't just about diet or exercise. Think about the caveman, sitting around the fire and:

- waiting to hunt, resisting the impulse to attack prey prematurely.
- making tools, focusing step-by-step for future use.
- navigating social scenarios, fitting in with the tribe through learned behaviors.

This ability to plan ahead and control impulses offered a distinct survival edge, eventually becoming hardwired into our brains. And **here's the kicker!** Studies support this, suggesting that the advanced human prefrontal cortex evolved precisely to handle these tasks.

"What we call self-control has evolved to be the lighthouse guiding our ship in the swirl of life's immediate gratifications and long-term goals."

Our brains are skillfully wired to harness these tendencies. The interplay between the prefrontal cortex and neurotransmitters shares a well-choreographed balance to maintain willpower. Evolution patiently shaped this ability, ensuring our forebears and us too...flourish in complex, uncertain environments.

So next time you feel like giving in to an impulsive decision, remember that your brain—complex and wonderfully capable—is designed to help you navigate the challenges of self-control. Whether it's resisting a tempting dessert or sticking to a workout routine, from the cave days to today's busy world, your body and mind are on your side.

How Willpower Works in the Brain

Ever wondered what's happening up there when you're trying to resist that cookie or push yourself to go to the gym? It's fascinating stuff, really. Our brains hold the key to understanding willpower, and it all revolves around decision-making. When you're making decisions, your brain is like the juggler at a circus – constantly balancing and coordinating. There's this part of the brain, the prefrontal cortex, that's kind of like the ringleader. It's responsible for planning, controlling impulses, and setting goals.

Now, let's add another layer to this. The prefrontal cortex has a challenging job and it's fueled by glucose. Yeah, the same stuff that's in sugary snacks. Glucose is like the brain's gasoline – it powers all these mental activities. Without enough fuel, it's like trying to drive a car on fumes. You've probably noticed that when you're super tired or hungry, making good choices is *that* much harder. Turns out, that's because with low glucose levels, the prefrontal cortex doesn't function as well. This can leave you feeling kind of *meh* about sticking to your good habits.

It's not all problematic though! Just like you can build muscle with regular exercise, you can also build willpower through practice. Imagine learning to play the piano; at first, it's tricky, but practice makes those muscle memories kick in, right? Willpower operates a bit like a muscle – the more you use it, the stronger it gets. You want proof? Studies have shown that small, regular acts of self-control (such as keeping a tidy desk or committing to a simple diet rule), can actually improve overall willpower.

So, let's toss in a practical example for good measure. Recall the last time you said "no" to that tempting cookie after dinner? It might have felt tough, but what you did was give your willpower a little workout. And as you keep flexing that self-control muscle, it will indeed get stronger. Just remember, it's the small, consistent efforts that add up.

Here's a nugget of wisdom about energy and willpower:

"The more often you resist something tempting, the more energy and focus you'll have for the next challenge."

Energy depletion is a real deal. When you exert a lot of energy making decisions throughout the day, you can experience what experts call decision fatigue. Ever found yourself unable to decide what to eat for dinner after an exhausting day? That's it – decision fatigue. By evening, your brain is tired and short on glucose, making simple choices frustratingly difficult. This reinforces why a balanced diet and proper rest are indispensable.

But, think practice makes perfect? Maybe not perfect, but pretty darn good! Sure, these new habits could be hard initially, but that's only because your brain isn't wired for them yet. With time, patience, and regular practice, it rewires – creating new pathways that make disciplined choices easier.

Remember those superheroes with incredible willpower? Often, they're depicted training rigorously, doing seemingly minute tasks to keep their skills sharp. Think of your willpower in a similar fashion.

- **Compassionate Self-Control**: Be kind to yourself.
- **Mindfulness**: Stay aware of your actions and decisions.
- **Routine Practice**: Consistent small efforts pay off.

Your brain is fascinating! With daily small steps and an understanding of your brain's fuel, you'll get better and better at mastering your willpower. It's all about the training!

The Role of Emotions in Self-Discipline

Emotions play a big part in our ability to maintain **self-discipline**. It might sound obvious, but managing how we feel can seriously impact how we handle our goals and commitments. When we're in control of our emotions, it's easier to make good choices, stick to plans, and push through difficult times. This isn't about being emotionless - far from it! It's more about knowing when to let your emotions drive you and when to keep them in check.

Consider **emotional regulation**, which is like a superhero skill for self-discipline. It's what helps you stay calm and focused even when things are getting tough. Research shows that people who are better at managing their emotions tend to have greater self-control. For instance, when you're feeling really motivated and happy, you're likely to tackle tasks with more energy and enthusiasm. Conversely, if you're feeling overwhelmed or anxious, it can be easy to fall into procrastination or stress-eating.

That brings us to **emotional triggers**. These are those pesky little things that can challenge our self-control. For some of us, it might be stress from work that makes us want to binge on junk food. For others, feelings of boredom can lead to endless scrolling through social media, far away from productive activities. Knowing your triggers is the first step in fighting back. Imagine you're on a diet - knowing that stress leads to overeating helps you prepare healthier snacks ahead of time or find other ways to relax that don't involve food.

Now, managing emotions doesn't have to be complicated. There are simple techniques you can use every day. **Deep breathing**, for example, is incredibly effective. When you take slow, deep breaths, it actually tells your body to calm down. This can help you regain control in moments of intense emotion. Another technique is **mindfulness**, which is like a fancy word for paying attention to the present. If you find yourself distracted, just take a moment to recognize what you're feeling and why. Sometimes, acknowledging your emotions can help you gain power over them.

Sometimes, we think that toughing it out on our own is the best option, but sharing our feelings can actually be super helpful. Talking to a friend or even journaling your thoughts can provide clarity and release pent-up emotions. It's surprising how getting your thoughts out can lighten the mental load, making self-discipline feel less like a chore and more like a smooth ride.

Self-discipline isn't about destroying your emotions, it's about listening to the useful ones and managing the disruptive ones.

Setting small, achievable goals is another great way to manage emotions and enhance discipline. Large, daunting tasks can stir up feelings of worry or fear. By breaking them into smaller, bite-sized goals, not only does the work feel more manageable, but each small win boosts your confidence, creating a positive emotional cycle.

Don't beat yourself up when things don't go as planned—showing **self-compassion** is key. It's easy to fall into the trap of negative self-talk, but being kind to yourself during slip-ups helps you get back on track faster. We're all human, and perfection isn't the goal; progress is.

Little techniques make big differences. Whether it's practicing **gratitude**, engaging in **regular exercise**, or simply ensuring you get enough sleep, these habits can significantly improve your emotional well-being and, by extension, your self-discipline. Each time you manage your emotions instead of letting them control you, you strengthen your mental resilience, making future challenges that much easier to navigate.

Understanding the role of emotions in self-discipline helps transform fleeting motivation into enduring habits. So go ahead, breathe, reflect, share, and celebrate those small wins—you're equipped to take on the world.

Benefits of Positive Discipline on Mental Health

When we talk about positive discipline, one incredible benefit is how it can reduce anxiety and stress. You know that feeling when there's just too much piling on at once—school, friends, family... everything? Yeah, positive discipline helps with that. It's about setting boundaries for yourself, and it takes a huge load off your mind. You plan your day, set a goal, and stick to it—no more chaotic rush that leaves you frazzled. You might even say it feels like finding an unexpected sanctuary in the middle of a bustling city. **Stress and anxiety levels drop substantially** when you have a clear, disciplined approach—"like a personal roadmap guiding you through the whirlwind of daily life".

Another wonderful thing is how it improves resilience and coping skills. That time you dealt with something really tough and came out stronger? That's what we're talking about. Positive discipline builds that muscle. Imagine going through hard times but knowing you have the tools to handle it. It's not just surviving; it's thriving—but not in a canned, motivational poster kind of way. It feels authentic. When you're disciplined positively, you learn to handle setbacks (small or big) with more grace. You don't crumble under pressure; instead, you start seeing challenges as opportunities to grow. It's like training for a marathon (even if you hate running); every little practice session makes you tougher for the big race.

So here's another goodie: it tangibly enhances overall well-being and life satisfaction. Yes, really! Think about how satisfying it is to tick tasks off a list or hit a milestone you've been working toward. Positive discipline isn't about restricting yourself; it's about making decisions that lead to long-term happiness. It's knowing that saying no to another late-night series binge might suck *right* now, but morning-you will thank you for sticking to a healthy sleep routine. Over time, this kind of consistent behavior creates a snowball effect... suddenly, things aren't just bearable—they're genuinely good.

But there's more to it than just feeling less stressed or more resilient. Your overall mood lifts, and here's why: positive discipline creates a foundational sense of control in your life. When you have control, you have confidence. Imagine feeling at peace because you know you've got a handle on your commitments, aspirations, and even your chaos. This kind of mood lift isn't fleeting; it's the sort of change that sticks. You're happy because you chose what matters, and you stuck to it.

Here's the icing on the cake: with positive discipline, you sometimes get extra time to enjoy the fun parts of life without guilt. The lazy Sunday you didn't always have can become a regular feature—not just a fluke. Moments of rest and joy feel earned and fully indulged. It's a balance. You *earn* your downtime by effectively managing your day-to-day tasks. This approach transforms relaxation from "ahh, finally" to "see, this is the life."

So, in a nutshell, positive discipline touches every part of mental health. It provides a scaffold that reduces mental clutter, builds resilience, and cranks your satisfaction level up a few notches. Bam. Just like that. You take reins over your own happiness.

For those who love a bit of wisdom:

"Self-discipline is the magic that turns 'I'm trying' into 'I can'"

Practicing positive discipline may take effort, but it's a game-changer for your mind. Simple steps can spiral into monumental shifts—imagine a world where you cruise through your stress, handle setbacks, and actually enjoy the daily humdrum.

Chapter 2: The Psychology Behind Change

"Life is 10% what happens to us and 90% how we react to it."

Change isn't easy, and do we resist it. This chapter explores **why**. We're wired to stick with what we know—the comfortable status quo—even if it's not good for us. Ever wondered why you cling to old habits, even when you know you should change?

Overcoming Status Quo Bias sets the stage, digging into why we love staying put even when life's begging for an upgrade. Next, we tackle **Conquering Fear and Loss Aversion**. Fear often holds us back—doesn't it?—but understanding it can be your first step to conquering it.

In **Building Resilience Through Positive Thinking**, learn the art of bouncing back. It's not magic; it's mindset. This leads perfectly into **The Power of Mindset Shifts**, where you'll see how changing your perspective can change your life.

Creating a Vision for Personal Growth wraps things up, helping you look ahead with a clear goal in mind. Imagine becoming the best version of yourself—that's what this chapter aims to help you with.

Ready to dig in? Each section is crafted to **help you grow** and understand not just the psyche behind change, but how you can make it work for you.

Overcoming Status Quo Bias

Understanding the comfort of familiarity is honestly half the battle. I bet you know exactly what I mean – the snug feeling of your favorite worn-out sweatshirt, the same cozy spot on the couch every evening, or perhaps, the daily ritual of a steaming cup of coffee in the morning. These little pieces of comfy predictability add up, making you resistant to change, even when change might be good for you. The truth is, our brains are wired to find comfort in routines and familiarity. It's a survival tool: less unpredictability means less potential danger.

So, what's wrong with a little comfort? Maybe nothing... maybe everything. Consider this: you've got aspirations, dreams hanging out there in the distance. Things you really want but just can't seem to grab hold of. The comfort zone, lovely as it is, often keeps you from stretching out and making those dreams a reality.

To shift gears, **it's critical to identify and challenge automatic behaviors.** Those autopilot actions – the ones you don't even think about because they are so ingrained. Maybe you snooze the alarm multiple times each morning, or perhaps you always reach for your phone when you're stressed. These habits are second nature and breaking them feels like moving through molasses. It's no walk in the park. But here's what you need to do – start noticing. Begin with one or two small automatic behaviors. Take notes, observe, simply pay attention.

Once you've got a handle on your automatic responses, it's time for steps to initiate change with small actions... don't underestimate the power of tiny tweaks. Aim low and you'll hit the bullseye every time. Instead of a massive overhaul, consider altering one small part of your routine. A friend of mine, Sue, wanted to read more books – but she couldn't find the time. So she started reading one page a night. Just one page! Seems insignificant, doesn't it? But it worked. Before long, Sue was sailing through chapters. Baby steps push you forward gently, without the revolt that usually accompanies drastic changes.

"Small daily improvements over time lead to stunning results..."

A major benefit of starting small is that it plays nice with your brain's desire for familiarity. Taking baby steps does not shock the system; it simply nudges it. Soon enough, these small actions accumulate and you'll find your status quo slowly bending into a new shape.

Let's get a bit more practical:

- **Pick a habit:** Something small and easily doable – like drinking an extra glass of water a day. Sounds easy, right?
- **Set a trigger:** Choose a cue to prompt your new behavior. In Sue's case, she left her book on her nightstand.
- **Repeat:** Stick with the action daily, no matter what. Consistency breeds familiarity.

Every time you complete your chosen action, you're slowly rewiring your brain, shifting that once-entrenched status quo towards something new and beneficial. **Adopt the process**, little by little. It may seem small in the grand scheme, but each action towers in impact when viewed over time.

So, get out there and tweak... nudge... push just a tad. ---Tiny actions are seeds from which great changes can bloom. Be patient with yourself; enjoy these minor victories because together, they construct a new normal, one that's geared toward your dreams. **Stay resilient!**

Conquering Fear and Loss Aversion

Recognizing emotional barriers to change is the first step to conquering them. Many of us feel this invisible weight when faced with change—sometimes, it's this nagging feeling in the pit of your stomach or a voice in the back of your head urging you to stick to what's familiar. Change can be intimidating, and fear and loss aversion play huge roles in holding us back.

We've all been there: your brain focusing more on potential losses rather than gains. This natural bias predisposes us to resist choices that involve any risk. This is where reframing comes into play—turning that sense of dread into an exciting challenge. Whenever fear kicks in, **stop and assess**—what's the worst that could reasonably happen? And more importantly, what awesome opportunities might you miss out on if you never take the leap?

It's ironic, isn't it? That sometimes, the thing we're most afraid of is seldom as bad as it seems. Let's say you're considering quitting a job you dislike. Your fear screams at you about financial instability and the unknown. But look closer—could this actually be your ticket to a more fulfilling career? Look at change as a gateway, not as a dead-end.

One of the most effective ways to tackle loss aversion is through gradual exposure. Remember when you were a kid adapting to cold liquid? You'd start by dipping just a toe, then your feet, then, eventually, you're completely swimming without even noticing the cold. The same works with tough changes; start small—little steps towards what you're afraid to lose can steadily build up your comfort zone.

Handling fear doesn't always have to be dramatic. **Here's a thought process for you: Break your goals or challenges into bite-sized actions.** Afraid to start public speaking? Start by just speaking up a bit more in small gatherings. Instead of fixating on speaking to a hall of thousands, think of facing a smaller audience as slightly "touching your toes in the cold liquid".

Consider an everyday example: many people fear going to the gym because of potential embarrassment. They feel other people will judge them for not being as fit. Instead of jumping straight into a vigorous workout among seasoned gym-goers, just begin with smaller workouts at home, then progress to less crowded times at the gym. It's all about creating a sense of normalcy.

Let's be real; there's always going to be a fair share of self-doubt. The unknown is a big monster in our minds. **Breaking that monster down (small) bit by bit turns it into something conquerable**. This incremental strategy desensitizes our fear response, making stepping stones out of stumbling blocks. Sure, it takes time, but going at a manageable pace is more sustainable.

Like Yogi Berra once said:

"You can observe a lot just by watching."

The same applies to personal growth—see your emotional barriers as hurdles rather than brick walls. Watch how small adjustments bring you closer to where you want to be. Isn't it funny How tweaking your self-talk can make all the difference? "I could lose this" becomes, "I might gain so much."

In the big scheme of things, often the **small nudges** help us expand beyond our comfort zones more than seismic shifts. Taking charge of fear and loss aversion isn't about putting on a brave face and bearing it all but about understanding—then steadily overcoming—the obstacles inside us.

Building Resilience Through Positive Thinking

Let's not beat around the bush—keeping a positive outlook isn't just fluff. It's like... powerful stuff. When you're facing challenges (and let's face it, who isn't?), a good dose of optimism can truly make a difference. Good vibes work like a shield, helping you bounce back. Ever notice how people who seem cheerful just handle things better? It's like they have a secret weapon, and trust me, you can have that too.

An upbeat mindset comes with a full package of perks. For one thing, stress doesn't gnaw at you as much. Instead of freaking out, you might see problems as... hmm, how can we call them? Opportunities to grow. Sounds cheesy, but it's true. When you're not drowning in negative thoughts, everything—yes, even the annoying stuff—feels more manageable. Basically, enduring tough times becomes easier.

To stick to positivity like glue, cognitive strategies are your best buddies. Think about reframing. It's a fancy word for looking at things differently. Got a flat tire? Sure, you might be late, but maybe it's extra time to listen to that motivational podcast (or even sit back and have a mini re-set). Next up: visualization. Picture yourself nailing that project or winning that race. Your brain starts believing it and guess what? **You get more determined.**

Then, there's mindfulness. Pausing to concentrate on your breath, it's like hitting the refresh button on your mind. Makes keeping calm easier, I swear! Track all the good stuff happening. Got praise at work? Jotted it down. Ate a delicious meal? Appreciate each bite. Soon enough, you'll see positives sprouting everywhere!

For that extra oomph of daily positivity, use affirmations. Yep, talking to yourself isn't just for solving math problems out loud. You'd be astonished how reciting phrases like, "I am capable," or "Today is another chance to improve," uplifts you. Make it a habit—repeat them during your morning routine, or even as you're sipping coffee. These nuggets of enthusiasm do wonders for mental strength.

Need a bit of inspiration?

"The only limit to our realization of tomorrow will be our doubts of today. Let's move forward with strong and active faith."

Whenever you feel the negative tinge of self-doubt clawing at your heels, lean on those affirmations. Don't shove aside your talents or undermine your resilience. The mind absorbs... whatever it hears repeatedly. Fill it with positivity!

Positive thinking isn't a one-off; it's developed through practice. Like muscles you train at the gym, scratching the "same goes for the brain" isn't even needed—because, well, you know it's true. Commit to sparking optimistic thoughts and daily affirmations. Before long, your emotional resilience is skyrocketing through the roof.

To sum up, the life jackets of positive thoughts help... a lot. Staying optimistic reduces stress, and simple strategies like reframing, visualization, and mindfulness work wonders. Compliment these with meaningful daily affirmations, and you'll see the benefits blossoming around you. As awkward as it feels initially, give it a go—it could light up some surprising paths with miles of golden rays.

The Power of Mindset Shifts

It's amazing how powerful our mindset can be... I mean, think about it. The way we see ourselves and our abilities can change everything. You have probably heard about fixed and growth mindsets before, right? Well, the differences between them couldn't be bigger!

A **fixed mindset** assumes abilities and intelligence are static. It's like thinking, "I'm just not good at math" or "I'll never be able to run a marathon." People with this mindset believe talent alone creates success and forget the role effort plays. They shy away from challenges out of fear of failure, often saying "why bother if it's not my thing?" It can feel like they're stuck in the mud, unable to move forward.

Contrast that with a **growth mindset**! This one's a game-changer. It's the belief that abilities can be developed through dedication and hard work. Someone with a growth mindset embraces challenges and persists through setbacks. These individuals see failure not as a roadblock but as a springboard for growth. They'll say, "I might not be good at this… yet!"

Shifting to a growth-oriented perspective can feel like opening a new chapter in a story—exciting but a bit daunting. Here are a few techniques to adopt this perspective:

- **Reframe challenges** as opportunities. Instead of seeing a roadblock, look at it as a puzzle to solve.
- **Praise efforts, not just outcomes**. Focus on the learning process—this encourages continuous improvement.
- **Replace the word "failing" with "learning"**. When you stumble, tell yourself, "I'm learning!" (It really changes the vibe!)
- **Surround yourself with positivity**. Being around growth-minded individuals can seriously fuel your fire.

Starting to see the world differently all begins with a sprinkle of self-awareness—yes, just being aware of your thoughts can pave the way for massive shifts. When you catch yourself thinking, "I can't do this," pause. Notice that thought. Is it helping you?

Awareness acts like a mirror showing your true mindset. This insight gives you the power to pivot... to make conscious choices. It's like finding the light switch in a dark room. Boom—suddenly you see what you've been bumping into all this time. It's all about catching those negative thoughts and asking, "Is this the only truth? Or is there a different way to see this?"

An anecdote that always hits home for me is about a baker who nearly gave up her baking dreams because her cakes weren't initially winning contests. She realized that the fixed mindset was like a chain holding her down. Once she decided to focus on the process rather than just the prize, did things turn around! She started viewing each setback as a little lesson and each cake as a step closer to greatness.

Self-awareness isn't just about checking in with your thoughts... it's also about understanding your triggers and patterns. For instance, if you avoid new challenges at work because you doubt your abilities, recognizing this pattern is half the battle. Awareness is the engine driving mindset change.

Do not underestimate the sheer power of these shifts. They transform how you view effort, challenges, and setbacks. Imagine approaching each day with curiosity and eagerness rather than dread and doubt.

Mindsets shape whether we believe we can learn and change, or whether we see our limitations as fixed and permanent.

In closing, here's some food for thought: What small mindset shift could help you handle your next challenge better? Maybe it's as simple as viewing feedback as a tool for growth rather than as a personal attack. Little perspective tweaks like this might just lead to huge benefits. Shifting to a growth mindset might seem small, but, believe me, it can open up doors you never thought existed.

Creating a Vision for Personal Growth

Setting clear, achievable goals is like having a roadmap for where you want to go (though, in your mind, it's way cooler and filled with possibilities). Goals give you direction, purpose, and something concrete to work towards. When they're clearly defined and achievable, they help maintain focus and avoid distractions. Imagine the satisfaction of crossing off each milestone!

Now, visualization techniques... ah, these can truly shape your reality! By vividly picturing your success, you strengthen your commitment. It's not just a daydream; it's an intentional practice. Here's a fun tip: **try this every morning or before bed**. Close your eyes, take a few deep breaths, and picture yourself achieving that goal—every detail counts... the elation, the scene, even the smells if you can! The trick here is repetition because the more you visualize, the more you believe in your capability.

Here's a little anecdote: That time you desperately wanted something as a kid? Maybe it was a new toy or a trip to the amusement park. You'd think about it constantly, right? You'd tell your parents, your friends, doodle about it... persistently, until magic happened. Visualization isn't so different from that childlike enthusiasm and persistence. It nurtures the belief...

Moving on, creating a personal growth plan layers this vision with practicality. Personal growth plans are your detailed game plans—like layouts for a house you're building. And it needn't be complicated. Here's how you break it down:

- **Identify your core values** and passions. What are your non-negotiables? What makes you tick?
- **Set short-term and long-term goals** aligning with these values.
- **Action Plan**: Write actionable steps to reach these goals. Sometimes smaller steps work better.
- **Timeline**: Have a loose timeline but always flexible enough for adjustments.
- **Accountability**: Find a buddy or journal your progress.

It takes time to figure out your direction, and that's absolutely okay (patience is part of the process)!

"By failing to prepare, you are preparing to fail."

This quote always gives me a nudge whenever I feel overwhelmed by planning. It reiterates the necessity of having a structured plan to turn dreams into tangible outcomes.

To bless your plan with a personal touch, combine it with daily reflections. This can be achieved through journaling, setting aside 5-10 minutes daily to ponder:

- What worked today?
- What could be improved?
- How do I feel energy-wise?

Further, don't hesitate to tweak things... you learn so much about yourself and your sticking points through trial and error.

Personal growth isn't meant to be a huge, impossible leap; it's about steady, daily steps towards a better version of yourself. When goals are reality-checked, visualizations frequent, and plans snugly fit with one's values, the journey feels lighter, more enjoyable (and isn't that what we all crave deep down?).

The beauty of this approach is it can gently nudge you forward, rather than overwhelming you with unrealistic expectations. Making changes in small, digestible chunks builds confidence too. Before long, you'll be "wowing" yourself with progress!

Believe it, **you're much closer to the you-you-want-to-be than you think**...

Chapter 3: Core Principles of Mental Toughness

"There is no failure except in no longer trying."

Welcome to the heart of becoming truly tough—and not just in body, but in mind. In this chapter, we're exploring what it really means to have **mental toughness**. Ever wondered why some people sail through challenges, while others crumble? It all boils down to what's ticking in the brain.

Let's start simple: **Mental toughness** is like a muscle. You can strengthen it. (And yes, anyone can do it, even you.) We'll chat about how polishing those **executive functions** can make **decision-making** smoother and life, less stressful. Can't focus for more than a few minutes? Don't worry. Learn tricks to boost that **focus** and **concentration**!

Flexibility isn't just for gymnasts. **Cognitive flexibility** helps you think on your feet, adapt, and react better. **Impulse control** might sound boring, but it's a game-changer in making smart choices instead of quick, regrettable ones.

All this might sound a bit...laughable? But the benefits are huge. By the end, you'll have the tools to handle **stress**, make better decisions, and stay focused on what's important.

Ready to toughen up that mind? Turn the page and let's get started. This chapter is your ticket to a brighter, stronger brain!

What is Mental Toughness?

Mental toughness... it's more than just a catchy phrase—it's your secret weapon, your inner force driving you forward when the going gets tough. It's what helps you bounce back, stay calm, and steadfastly move toward your goals even when everything around you is going haywire.

That time you faced a big challenge and felt like giving up but didn't? That's resilience. Being resilient isn't about avoiding difficulties, it's about facing them head on. Maybe you were struggling at school, with never-ending assignments and mounting pressure, but you stuck it out and completed the semester (even when it felt like you were swimming upstream). That's the heart of resilience: grappling with challenges, learning from them, and becoming stronger as a result.

Commitment walks hand-in-hand with resilience but adds a bit more flavor. Think about how you've stuck with a childhood dream, something you've fantasized about for years (for me, it was writing this book!), and made slow, yet steady, progress. Commitment isn't flashy—it's often slow and sometimes a bit tedious, but every little bit counts. Envision walking across a tightrope... it's your dedication that keeps you balanced step by step. Most things worth having don't come instantly. We have to work for them, nurturing each small victory along the way.

Then there's maintaining *composure* under pressure. Imagine standing on a stage, heartbeat racing, palms sweaty (yes, even I've experienced this), and yet projecting confidence to the audience. That's mastering your emotions, compartmentalizing stress, and communicating effectively even when the world feels like it's spinning out of control. Think of a soccer goalie, calm and focused as the opponent rushes in to score. The ability to keep cool allows you to use your energy and your mind efficiently, ensuring you act, not just react.

But here's the kicker: you don't need to exhibit all-out bravado 24/7. Mental toughness is also about knowing when to give yourself a break and understanding your limits. Ever felt overwhelmed, took a deep breath, maybe a short walk, and came back with a fresher perspective? Practicing resilience, maintaining commitment, and composing yourself also balance with self-care and mindfulness. Occasionally, the bravest thing you can do is admit you need a pause.

So, what makes these elements stick? Let's boil it down to a few essentials:

- **Resilience**: Meeting challenges with a learning mindset,
- **Commitment**: Being in it for the long haul, even when the path gets rocky,
- **Composure**: Keeping cool and collected, no matter the external chaos.

One of the most memorable lines reinforcing these principles is:

"Success is not final, failure is not fatal: it is the courage to continue that counts."

We've all been there... facing a seemingly insurmountable obstacle, driven by an audacious goal, and needing to keep our cool while juggling it all. How you bounce back, stay steady, and hold your ground shapes not just your success story—but also the person you become along the way.

Everybody can cruise on a sunny day, but it's battling through the storms that builds that inner fortitude. It's grit. It's the unwritten rule of life—**resilience, commitment, and composure** ensure the journey is meaningful, engaging, and ultimately more rewarding.

Strengthening Executive Functions

When it comes to mental toughness, one major part we need to focus on is how we strengthen our executive functions. Let's begin by talking about **time management skills**. You ever find yourself wondering where the time went during the day? It happens to all of us, especially when we're juggling work, family, and maybe even a little bit of personal downtime. The key, though, is being intentional with your time. Think of time as a budget – you wouldn't just spend money randomly, right?

A handy trick I use is breaking the day into **blocks** of time. Between 8 AM to 9 AM, focus on checking emails and planning your day – no multitasking! You'll get more done and feel less scattered. Simple things like setting a timer or prioritizing tasks you hate doing (you know, get them over with) can make a real difference. And honestly, who doesn't love checking something off a to-do list?

Next, let's chew the fat on **goal-setting techniques**. Setting goals is like constructing a roadmap – if you don't know where you're going, any road will take you there. It's pretty remarkable what happens when you move beyond saying "I want to get fit" to defining "I want to run 5 miles without stopping in 3 months." Feeling specific? Awesome – it gives you a tangible target to aim for. SMART goals (Specific, Measurable, Achievable, Relevant, Time-bound), although you've likely heard of them, really do wonders.

Using real-life goals as examples, perhaps you decide you want to write a book. Instead of saying, "I'll write when I have time," try saying, "I'll write 500 words every day between 7 PM and 8 PM." Giving yourself specific directions makes the end results habit driven. Not to put too fine a point on it, but consistency is key here. By setting small, incremental goals, you'll find yourself gaining momentum. And once you're on that roll, it feels like magic, honestly.

Speaking of magic – or rather decision-making, the process we use can really break or make our willpower. It's like a muscle that gets stronger the more we practice, which brings me to an important point: **decisiveness**. It's so easy to get lost in analysis paralysis – too many options can actually be as daunting as too few. A piece of advice? Trust your intuition sometimes. Have criteria in place for decisions, like considering the potential long-term impact over short-term gains.

When it comes to goal setting, one successful individual once said:

"Goals are dreams with deadlines."

If that doesn't speak volumes about planning and executing effectively, I don't know what does. Decisiveness isn't just about making quick calls but making rightly-informed choices consistently and without too much second-guessing.

Lastly (without actually saying 'lastly'), let's just put this out there: managing one's life like this takes practice. And maturity. Failures will happen – because hey, we're all human. It's not whether those failures occur but how you respond to them. Missed a writing session? No sweat, pick it up the next day, review what distracted you, and adjust accordingly the next time.

We're all in this boat together, trying techniques to better ourselves—sharing these small changes can link us together in our quest to improve mental toughness. By bolstering our executive functions through improved time management, specific goal-setting, and sound decision-making, we navigate our lives with far more confidence and less struggle. Cheers to making those changes!

The Importance of Focus and Concentration

In today's hectic world, focusing can be a real challenge. "This distraction-filled world", I often think to myself, makes it tough to zero in on what's important. As we aim to build our mental toughness, it's clear that **eliminating distractions**, practicing mindfulness, and prioritizing tasks effectively are key.

We live in a noisy world full of gadgets demanding our attention – it's like a constant tug-of-war. Eliminating distractions can seem daunting, but trust me, it's worth it. When we carve out time for focused work, we discover that a quiet space delivers powerful results! To get started:

- **Identify distractions**: Think of what's commonly grabbing your attention away from the task at hand. Is it your phone, or maybe a cluttered workspace?
- **Set aside distraction-free periods**: Maybe it's an hour in the morning or just 15 minutes before bed. Having a designated distraction-free slot can work wonders.
- **Create a tidy workspace**: A clear desk helps you maintain a clear mind.

Just a little effort here goes a long way. You'll notice how your brain thanks you with sharper clarity and enhanced productivity.

Moving on, let's touch a bit on the practice of mindfulness. Now, I don't mean you need to meditate for hours – even a few minutes can make a difference. Practicing mindfulness means being present and actively engaged.

Think of it this way: you're reading this, and realizing your mind has wandered. That's okay! Just gently bring it back, refocus on these words... and there you go, you just practiced some mindfulness!

Mindfulness isn't about sitting with your eyes closed – it's about making a habit of bringing your mind back when it strays. Breathing deeply, slowing your thoughts, appreciating a calm moment – it all counts. This power of being present spills over into our ability to concentrate when it really matters.

Prioritizing tasks – another biggie – ties everything together. We can't do everything at once, can we? So let's be smart about it. Here are some tips:

- **Make a list**: Write down your tasks; seeing them on paper helps.
- **Rank by importance**: Tackle the most important (or toughest) one first... you'll feel a rush of satisfaction ticking it off.
- **Chunk big tasks**: Breaking down a daunting task into smaller steps makes it manageable.

Focus on this: "Done is better than perfect." Sometimes aiming for perfection can be our biggest distraction.

To put it simply, focusing isn't about juggling many things badly but handling a few things thoroughly. In the words of that wise someone: > "The ability to simplify means to eliminate the unnecessary so that the necessary may speak."

So, there we have it – distractions diminished, minds mindful, and tasks prioritized. It's all about giving ourselves the strongest foot forward. Trust in the process... we're on this path together. Each step brings the power of positive self-discipline closer, and in doing these steps, who knows? We all might find life a bit simpler and a lot more fulfilling.

Developing Cognitive Flexibility

Adapting to new situations... it's a skill we've all needed, especially during unpredictable times. You or maybe someone you know might have had to switch jobs or learn how to homeschool overnight. One thing's clear: being able to shift gears smoothly is essential. This is where **cognitive flexibility** shines—it's our ability to switch between thinking about multiple concepts or to think about several concepts simultaneously.

Consider when you've tried a new hobby or found yourself in an unfamiliar environment. How challenging can it be at first? Maybe you've relocated to a new city, and every street seemed like a maze. Each turn brings something new and unfamiliar. But, over time, these streets aren't so confusing anymore, right? That's adaptability at work.

In social situations, adapting isn't just about environments but also understanding different perspectives. When your friend sees a situation differently than you do, it's tempting to argue. But stepping back and considering their viewpoint not only broadens your horizon but sharpens your skill to see things from various angles. I recall a time when someone offered one viewpoint that completely floored me... never would have thought about it that way! Accepting diverse perspectives doesn't mean you have to agree—it means understanding that multiple truths can exist simultaneously.

Problem-solving creatively is another pillar of mental toughness. Here's where we get crafty. When faced with a problem, think of it like unscrewing a tightly sealed jar—a brute force might not always work; sometimes, tapping the side loosens things up. I've often noticed that stepping back (often literally) from a problem allows fresh ideas to seep in. Can you remember being stuck on a puzzle or tricky task at work, only to solve it when distracted by something else later?

Consider this, "When we are no longer able to change a situation, we are challenged to change ourselves." Doesn't that resonate? Life often hands us lemons, not a blueprint. Being flexible mentally equips us to make the best lemonade possible.

Over the years, I've developed some go-to strategies:

- **Mindfulness**: Taking a breath, slowing down that racing mind can do wonders. Puts you in the driver's seat of your thoughts.
- **Feedback Loop**: Engaging with others, enlightening. Feedback isn't criticism—it's growth nuggets.
- **Set Small Goals**: Sure, big goals are important, but chunking them down makes them less daunting and more achievable.

So, think about this: if every twist and turn in your life were predictable, it would... well, it would be dull! The magic happens when you negotiate unfamiliar paths with a calm mind, see angles invisible to rigid thinkers, and untangle problems with a creative flair.

Take your next twist in life head-on with this fresh lens. An open mind fights frustration. See beyond obstacles by exploring new ways constantly. And above all, cherish your unique ability to move through uncertainty with creativity!

Just keeping it light and stress-free helps. Stay open. Stay adaptable. Self-discipline isn't about being a hard taskmaster—it's about being a wise, gentle guide nudging oneself towards bigger, richer experiences.

Enhancing Impulse Control

Every day, we're faced with choices. Whether it's indulging in a treat or sticking to our goals, our ability to control impulses plays an essential role. The art of delaying gratification is one of the jewels of impulse control. Think about a time when sticking to a long-term goal paid off... wasn't it worth it? When you take a step back and remember the joy of accomplishing something significant, it makes those small temptations seem far less alluring.

One technique to implement delayed gratification is setting up mini-rewards. Let's say you have a task that can be done in chunks. Reward yourself after each mini-accomplishment—a long stroll in the park, a favorite snack, or even a quick nap. These little rewards make it easier to hold off on the bigger, more immediate satisfactions.

Stress is another major player when it comes to impulse control. When we're stressed, our capacity to stick to our goals dims because we often look for quick fixes to make ourselves feel better. Stress management, thus, becomes vital. Engaging in mindfulness activities like deep breathing or even yoga can be incredibly beneficial. Personally, whenever things get overwhelming, a few minutes of deep breathing feels like hitting the reset button on my stress levels.

Taking breaks is another solid stress management strategy. Break your tasks into smaller portions, and take a conscious break in between to recharge. This isn't just idle time – it's purposefully giving your brain some rest. It's like doing reps at the gym; your muscles need short rests in between for maximum efficacy.

Managing our emotions also links deeply with impulse control. Something as simple as identifying what you're feeling can drop stress levels significantly. When you're able to put words to your emotions, they seem less daunting... Knowing you're angry or anxious facilitates better management.

For a more tangible takeaway, let's look into emotional regulation practices:

- *Journaling regularly*: emptying your thoughts onto paper can provide clarity. It not only helps you identify triggers but also navigate through them constructively.
- *Exercise*: Whenever you move your body, yet another avenue for emotional release opens. You don't have to do a marathon; even a 20-minute walk does wonders.

- *Listening to music*: choose songs that match—or transform—your mood. Feeling blue? Music can be an incredible companion. While this may sound trivial, learning to align your feelings this way provides an unexpected emotional buffer.

Let's crack open a bit of wisdom on the subject:

"The greatest wealth is to live content with little, for there is never want where the mind is satisfied."

This couldn't be more relevant when it comes to impulse control. Satisfying the mind doesn't just happen; it's nurtured through conscious effort and strategies.

Ultimately, mastering impulse control through delayed gratification, stress management, and emotional regulation isn't about being unemotional or robot-like. It's about acknowledging that the small steps you take add up, aren't they? It's about allowing these principles to morph into second nature, and the next time you're faced with a tempting impulse, your parlor tricks will seem a lot more enticing... won't they?

So, next time a challenge looms, remember—it's within these small choices and habits that your fortress of mental toughness is built. Just consider the possibilities when these techniques blend seamlessly into your daily life!

Part 2: Preparing for Success

Chapter 4: Setting Goals with Intention.

"Setting goals is the **first** step in turning the invisible into the visible."

In this chapter, we'll uncover the secret sauce behind setting **meaningful** goals and doing it with **intention**. Have you ever wondered why some goals remain out of reach, while others seem to turn into reality effortlessly? The difference often lies in the details—how you plan, visualize, and tackle obstacles along the way.

We all know how frustrating it can be to set goals and fail to meet them. This can leave you feeling discouraged or not good enough. But here's the good news: There are tried-and-true methods to keep you on track. We'll explore crafting SMART goals for laser-focused success and delve into visualization techniques that bring clarity. Ever heard of the WOOP method? It's an amazing approach to overcoming hurdles (whether big or small). Then there's the GROW model—a handy guideline to align your efforts with your intentions.

By the end of this chapter, expect to feel empowered and equipped to set achievable goals. Your path awaits, paved with affirmations and positive reinforcement. Ready to transform your aspirations? Flip the page, and let's set fantastic goals together!

Crafting SMART Goals for Success

Specific, measurable, achievable, relevant, and time-bound—the golden recipe for crafting goals that actually mean something. Setting goals isn't just about what you want but defining a clear path to get there. **Specific** goals shine because well, they're not hazy. They paint a vivid picture, and yes, details matter. Think of it like choosing an exact spot on the map, instead of saying, "I want to get somewhere nice."

So how do we make them specific? Instead of settling with "I want to exercise more," go with, "I want to jog for 30 minutes every morning." Feel the difference? We'll get to it step-by-step:

Be Specific

Your goals need clarity. Rather than a blurry vision, you require sharp, crystal-clear targets. If you aim to read more, avoid the vague and go sharper—state how many books you want, their genres, maybe even how long you'll spend reading each day. Don't just say, "get healthy." Replace it with, "lose 10 pounds by eating more vegetables, avoiding sugary drinks, and working out thrice a week."

Specific goals give you a defined target to aim for, making you aware of what you need to do daily. Missing specifics is like shooting arrows in the dark, hoping one hits the bullseye.

Make It Measurable

If you can't measure your success, you won't know when you get there. Progress needs numbers...it needs checkboxes. Like for losing weight, isn't it simpler saying, "I aim to lose 2 pounds in a month" instead of "just lose weight"? Metrics guide us through the struggles and triumphs, showing us how far we've come and what's left to conquer—bits and pieces we can track and celebrate.

"To measure is to know," keeps echoing in my mind (and no, it wasn't Einstein who said that).

Keep It Achievable

Ambition is great, but your goals should not be castles in the sky. Aim high, but keep your feet on the ground (a little patience goes a long way). Ask yourself: Is this goal within my reach? If not, tweak it. Instead of thinking, "I'll run a marathon next month," try, "I'll prepare by running three miles, five times a week, for the next two months." Small, realistic steps—they build confidence, trust me.

Make Your Goals Relevant

Do your goals align with your core values? This is where the heart comes in. Your goals must resonate with who you are and what you believe. Let's say you value community and health—joining a local football team rather than aiming for solo gym sessions might be more up your alley. Goals should fuel your purpose, push you to grow in areas that matter most to you.

Evaluate constantly if achieving this goal steers you closer to your life's tune.

Define Your Time Boundaries

Deadlines give a sense of urgency and motivation. A time frame isn't about rushing; it's about giving your goal a lifespan. It's about creating a sense of significance—turning abstract desires into realities bounded by a date. Make that clarity pop...don't just say, "I want to learn Spanish"; set the deadline. "Enroll in a language course and hold a full conversation by December 30."

Pinned goals lead to finished tasks.

Creating **SMART** goals is an art. With specificity, you set a clearing in your forest; with measurability, you map your path; with attainability, you resolve to walk that path—and relevancy, keeps your journey illuminated...add the timer, and you're hitting the ground running.

Visualization Techniques for Clarity

When talking about achieving goals, the magic of visualization is priceless. Anytime we hear about athletes breaking records or entrepreneurs building empire… they most likely visualized their success. It's like dreaming while being fully awake, creating a mental movie. Let's see how we can use this "secret weapon."

The **trick** is mental imagery. This may sound fancy, but it's really simple. Close your eyes and **picture yourself hitting your goal**. Think of the last time you really wanted something meaningful— c'mon, picture it clearly in your mind. See yourself reaching that desire, living the moment as if it's happening now.

Then, get into sensory details. Pay attention here because it's not only about seeing—it's feeling, hearing, maybe even smelling it. For instance, let's say your target is completing a marathon. See yourself crossing the finish line… feel the strength in your legs, hear the crowd cheering, maybe even sense the scent of the fresh grass (or the less fresh smell of sweat all around you!). Each of these tiny details connects more to the real experience, making it more powerful and, frankly, more enjoyable. These are not sterile images but vibrant scenes.

Next comes the emotional connection. This part brings it all together. You wanna "feel" success in your imagination as deeply as if it's really happening. Feel the joy—grab on tight to that excitement and pride, perhaps even relief you'd feel upon achieving your marathon sign-off, bagging your dream job or maybe seeing your small side hustle turn big. Think beyond—how will others react? Will you feel lighter?

Now, let's put it all together through steps that matter the most.

- **Find a Quiet Space**

Begin in a calm environment where distractions can't reach you (perhaps a comfy corner at home or your favourite park).

- **Relax Your Mind and Body**

Take several deep breaths to relax. Calmness helps you focus better.

- **Picture Your Goal**

Here is the kicker... see yourself in full action achieving that goal. If your goal is perhaps public speaking, imagine being on stage, every pair of eyes on you, showcasing your best.

"There's power in connecting your dreams with emotion and connecting illusion with all your senses, turning imagination into "a movie" where you frame your own success."

- **Engage All Your Senses**

Don't cheat yourself, bring in sounds, sights, touches, even tastes and smells if you can. This could be hearing the audience's applause, feeling the warmth of spotlights or tasting that victory candy (yum M&Ms anyone?).

- **Feel the Emotions Intensively**

Mary, who imagined herself acing her job interview, felt the exhilaration right through... "legendary joy and the profound relief" are thoughts that surrounded her and kept her pushing for the best.

When you cure yourself in imagination, with all sensory details ticking, you feel it with every pore. Feel that success like it's happening... because often?

Setting goals with intention through these powerful ingredients doesn't only set compasses right but engrains confidence that **shaking hands become strong, hesitant words bold, and unclear pathways smoother**

So, with that, next time remember to cross your finish line, stand victorious on your mental images!

WOOP Method: Wish, Outcome, Obstacle, Plan

Sometimes, the hardest part of achieving our goals is figuring out where to start. Here's where the **WOOP method** comes in—a little tool that's simple and wildly effective. Let's get into how it works.

Step 1: Wish

Start with your deepest, most genuine aspiration. What do you want to achieve? Maybe it's learning a new skill, like baking the perfect apple pie. Or perhaps it's something broader, like spending more quality time with family. Think big but also be realistic. A wish like "I want to bake the best apple pie" is heartfelt and tangible, unlike declaring you're going to win the Great British Bake-Off right away. (Trust me, focusing on smaller, more manageable wishes sets you up for better success.)

Step 2: Outcome

This is where you get to daydream, a little. Envisioning your success can be quite fun, actually. Imagine your wish fulfilled—those golden apple pies coming out of the oven, the house filled with an amazing scent, and your family gathered around the table eagerly waiting to dig in. How does that make you feel? What does success look like? Let your mind play out every rich detail... the compliments, the happiness. It's like composing a mental snapshot of victory.

Sometimes, we need a powerful reminder of what's possible.

"A journey of a thousand miles begins with a single step."

Your small wish, baked pie or quality time, can be that first step. Visualizing this success can light a fire within you.

Step 3: Obstacle

"Here's where things get real," you might think. And you're right. Identify what's standing in your way. Recognize the practical barriers you're facing. Maybe it's the lack of good recipes or, possibly, oven settings that intimidate you. Sometimes time management is the big issue—like, how do you fit this into your busy week? These obstacles aren't there to discourage you; rather, seeing them clearly helps you prepare. When you anticipate that your problem might be finding the best ingredients, you'll also know what you need to address, without those side glances that "surprised" barriers often invoke.

Step 4: Plan

Alright, so it's not about a perfectly mapped out Roman Empire road here. It's about feasible actions that keep you moving forward.

Consider these practical steps:

- **Identify Resources**: Maybe you search for reliable recipes on trusted food blogs.
- **Allocating Time**: How about picking a quiet Sunday afternoon for pie-baking, when distractions are minimal?
- **Ask for Help**: Don't hesitate to ask a friend or family member who's a pie-pro to give you some tips!

Keep in mind there's no single perfect path. Flexibility is key. Strategies might require a tweak here or there. After all, distractions are part of the process, too, making strategic pivots essential.

Use techniques like WOOP to create a personal plan.

By putting effort into defining real wishes, visualizing the outs, planning actionable steps for obstacles that arise, you step into empowering territory. And Yes, these steps not only drive goals but help pave smarter paths through life's spontaneous shifts. The beauty of approaching goals this way serves as both preparation and optimism-in-action... not only enhancing end results but adding resplendent purpose along each step.

Using the GROW Model to Achieve Goals

When we're setting goals, having a clear-eyed approach can make all the difference between excitement and frustration. Here's where the **GROW model** comes in—**Goal, Reality, Options, Will**. Simple words, but powerful when brought together. Let's dive right into using this tool effectively in our daily lives to hit those targets with intention.

So, you're thinking about your objectives. Setting a goal should stir something inside you—a sense of excitement or even a small flutter of nervousness. Perhaps you want to run a marathon or start a new business? Whatever it is, **making the goal specific and measurable is key**. Imagine running into a friend in six months; what would you tell them you accomplished? Did you lose 15 pounds or finish reading 20 books? Specifics anchor your efforts.

But before leaping into action, take a hard look at your **Reality**. Assess where you stand right now. It's like trying to build a house on shifting sand—you've got to know your foundation first. Are there habits or beliefs holding you back? Sometimes revealing these can sting a bit. One might discover, for instance, that time management is a weak spot. Maybe you spend hours on social media (don't we all, sigh)? In any case, the point is to be brutally honest with yourself. "Pep talks" are good, but insights are better.

Once you've got a grip on your current situation, dream up your **Options**. This is where the fun begins because the possibilities start to form. You can kick the Why and How questions around like a soccer ball with friends at the park. "Why do I want to run a marathon?" "How can I fit training into my weekly schedule?" The mind loves these questions—they get your creative juices flowing. Would joining a local running club inspire your progress? Maybe a personal trainer isn't a bad idea? Listing these choices illuminates paths you didn't consider before.

Alright, time to zero in on **Will**. This isn't about sheer effort. It's a considered commitment. What actions resonate with you? Start by picking the options that feel right; these are often the most sustainable. If a run with that local club excites you more than solitary jogs, that's the winner. Write down your steps. An anecdote for you: I've seen a friend who decided to write daily... not because it was easy, but affirmative will led her fingers to keys, and pages flowed. She took charge, one short writing session at a time, making little consistent wins until one day, there was a book!

As we're wrapping this up, let's remind ourselves that goals should always be attached to intentions. Success isn't an accident; it's the sum of purposeful actions grounded in your values. Here's something that sums it up beautifully:

"The best way to predict your future is to create it."

That's you, stepping into each action with clarity and intention. It's all within your grasp if you align your willpower with a clear assessment of your reality and get creative with your options. Go make something amazing happen!

In practical terms:

- **Death by bulletpoints? Never! Less is more. Meaningful context only.**
- Anchor your **goal** with specifics.
- Face your **reality** honestly, it saves disappointment later.
- Stack your mental "toolbox" with **options** abound.
- **Will** it into action with steps you believe in.

Empower yourself with the GROW model. Write it down. Internalize it. And make these steps second nature. On to your next goal with purpose and joy—you've got what it takes!

Affirmations and Positive Reinforcement

Daily affirmations—just two small words that pack such a punch. They may seem a bit corny at first, but trust me, they work. Starting the day with positive talk shapes your mindset—"I am capable," "I can handle whatever comes," and "I have the tools to succeed." These words, spoken to your reflection every morning, begin to integrate into your very being, boosting your self-confidence bit by bit. Think of affirmations as mental fuel—a small dose can uplift your spirit and keep you charging forward.

When you were a kid and completed a difficult task, how fantastic did you feel when someone cheered you on—"Great job!" or "You did it!" Now, imagine using that same principle as an adult, encouraging yourself with positive self-talk to power through challenges. Whenever you face adversity, say, during a rough day at work or when preparing for a presentation… whisper some uplifting words to yourself. Positive self-talk isn't just about feeling good; it builds resilience. Reminding yourself that you're strong and capable can make a world of difference when you're going through tough times.

Let's talk about those small wins too. Ah, the joy of milestones reached—these shouldn't be passed over lightly. Breaking larger goals into smaller steps—baby steps, if you will—and celebrating those builds momentum. Finished a project ahead of schedule? Treat yourself to something fun. It doesn't have to be grand. Even a nice meal, some time off, or that book you've been eyeing works. Rewarding milestones reinforces your hard work and keeps the eyes on the prize. These rewards are more than just indulgences—they signal to your brain that progress is being made and success is within reach.

Step 1: Start with Daily Affirmations

Each morning, take a few minutes for yourself—stand tall, look in the mirror, and seed positivity in your mind:

- "I am confident."
- "Every day, in every way, I'm getting better and better."

Do it until it becomes second nature... it won't happen overnight, but stick with it. Over time, these affirmations form a resilient fortress around you.

Step 2: Practice Positive Self-Talk

Find yourself in a rough spot? Wondering if you'll ever get through? Pause and play cheerleader:

- "I've got this under control."
- "I've handled worse and come out fine."

It may feel silly, but hearing your own voice telling you to keep pushing can be enormously reassuring. Try writing these down too; seeing them in black and white can make them more tangible.

Step 3: Reward Milestones

Set small, manageable goals along the way to big achievements. Here's how:

- If you finish a part of a big project, reward that success.
- Didn't give in to procrastination for a whole week? Treat yourself.

These rewards don't have to break the bank—a favorite snack, an episode of a beloved show, or just some downtime.

To further stress the best approach:

"Your mind will always believe everything you tell it. Feed it faith. Feed it truth. Feed it with love."

Do this consistently, make it a habit, and witness the gradual yet powerful changes unfold.

Often, people wait for a grand success to celebrate bliss, ignoring these simple acts of self-care that catalyse greater self-discipline. Small, incremental steps and positive reinforcements have a magic to them—a magic that keeps the motor running and spirits high.

So, wake up tomorrow with purpose, talk to yourself with kindness, and remember—it's okay, rather, necessary to celebrate even the smallest of victories. They all add up.

Let's Get Practical!

Welcome! Ready to take what you've learned about setting goals with intention and put it into action? Great! Stick with me, we're going to turn those abstract ideas into some solid steps you can **practically** follow. Imagine we're having a friendly chat while we build this together.

Step 1: Set a SMART Goal

Alright, the *initial step* is about creating a SMART goal—Specific, Measurable, Achievable, Relevant, and Time-bound. It's easy to say "I want to be healthy," but that's super vague, right? Let's sharpen it up. Suppose your goal is to run a 5K race in three months. Let's break it down:

- **Specific**: "I will run a 5K race"
- **Measurable**: "I will measure my progress by how far and fast I can run"
- **Achievable**: "I've started running recently, and building up to 5K in three months is doable"
- **Relevant**: "I want to improve my fitness level"
- **Time-bound**: "In three months"

So, your SMART goal sounds like this: "I will run a 5K race in three months, measuring my progress each week to improve my fitness level."

Say it out loud to really get it to stick in your head! Doesn't that feel more real now?

Step 2: Visualization Techniques for Clarity

Time to close your eyes—or you know, just find a peaceful spot. Think about successfully running that 5K race. Picture the path ahead of you, feel the rhythm of your feet hitting the pavement, hear the cheers at the finish line... Maybe even break a little sweat just imagining it.

By visualizing your successful run, you are giving your mind a clear picture to aim for. Trust me, this sense of clarity gives you a boost to mentally prepare.

Step 3: Apply the WOOP Method

Next up, let's tackle this with the WOOP method: Wish, Outcome, Obstacle, Plan. Simple, yet super effective...

- **Wish**: To run a 5K in three months.
- **Outcome**: Feel accomplished, hits a significant fitness milestone.
- **Obstacle**: Lack of motivation on busy days (sound familiar?), potential muscle soreness.
- **Plan**: Tackle lack of motivation by joining a running group or using a running app for accountability; stretching and proper warm-up to manage soreness.

Write these down. When your obstacles rear their heads, you'll know exactly what to do.

Step 4: Using the GROW Model

Let's further strategize using the GROW model: Goal, Reality, Options, and Will.

- **Goal**: You've got it—run that 5K.
- **Reality**: Okay, where are you now? Perhaps you can run 1K comfortably. No biggie, it's a starting point.

- **Options**: Could include joining a local running club, scheduling regular runs, or getting a buddy involved for some mutual support.
- **Will**: Define the steps, maybe "I will run three times a week, gradually increasing my distance," with regular check-ins on your progress.

Lay it out clearly so you're always aware of your game plan.

Step 5: Affirmations and Positive Reinforcement

This step is all about talking to yourself—seriously. Start your day with: "I am a committed runner. Every day, I get closer to running a 5K". Post it on your wall if you have to. Positive vibes are infectious.

And hey, give yourself rewards for those mini-milestones. Ran two kilometers without stopping? Treat yourself to something special, maybe some new running gear!

Wrap-Up

Phew! Look at what you've done: you set a **SMART goal**, visualized it, mapped out your **WOOP**, dug deep with the **GROW model**, and wrapped yourself in positive affirmations. These steps stitch together all the key lessons of setting intentional goals and conveying a personal touch and sense of realism to it.

Try this out—step by step. You'll feel less lost, and more like you're casually chatting your way to success with an old friend guiding the way. Now, lace up those shoes and hit the track!

The most critical point here is consistency and effort. Times where you will feel like taking a break or giving up can happen often and the greatest way against fighting it is to always remember this written game plan you have follow it strictly and measure your progress. Small consistent steps go a long way!

Chapter 5: Building Effective Habits.

"Chains of habit are too light to be felt until they are too heavy to be broken."

Welcome to a turning point in our book—**Building Effective Habits**. This chapter is crucial because without the right habits, it's hard to make lasting changes, isn't it? You'll find yourself falling back into old patterns, despite the best-intended goals. So buckle up, because here we go.

Have you ever thought why some routines stick while others fizzle out? It's no mystery; it's science. In **Habit Stacking for Long-Term Success**, you'll join a step-by-step guide to pile up small habits that can grow into life-changing routines. Simple strategies can lead to enormous success... Imagine what that could look like for you!

Your **Morning and Evening Routines** can be the secret sauces that set the tone for a fantastic day or help you wind down perfectly. Most people underestimate their power. But guess what— we're going to go through routines that actually *work*.

Short on time but long on stress? Learn how to integrate **Exercise and Meditation** into your day effortlessly. And it's not just about moving your body or focusing your mind... it's about *your* well-being.

Food is fuel, as you'll see in **Healthy Nutrition for Optimal Performance**. Feeling sluggish and low? Your nutrition could be the culprit. Eat right, perform right!

Lastly— ever felt cranky when you didn't sleep well? No mystery there, it's all about self-control. The **Role of Sleep in Building Willpower** takes a closer look at why your sleeping habits matter so much.

So why wait any longer? Jump in and find out how these insights can make your life smoother, healthier, and a lot more productive!

Habit Stacking for Long-Term Success

Creating powerful routines starts with the notion of combining small habits into a cohesive sequence. It might sound fancy, but stick with me—this approach to building habits can be super easy and effective. Imagine brushing your teeth... it's just one part of your morning. What if you could smoothly flow from brushing your teeth to doing something else beneficial without thinking much about it?

The key is to start with something really simple—something that you'd do daily without much effort. Brushing your teeth (yes, exactly!), having your morning coffee, or maybe tying your shoes. Think of it more as linking, rather than creating new and overwhelming tasks.

Identify Simple Daily Habits

Look around at the habits you do every single day. Make a list (you know pieces of paper? Handy!). Things like:

- Brushing your teeth
- Making coffee
- Taking a shower
- Putting on your shoes

Pick one of these as an anchor. For real success, it often works best to choose the one you enjoy or don't mind much. It's like adding riders onto an existing train... hopping on quite naturally really.

Add One Small, Easy Habit to Your Anchor

Let's say you want to start meditation but dread dedicating full time to it yet. Attach it to your coffee time.

"Take ten deep breaths immediately after you press the coffee machine button."

Easy right? The idea here is minimal extra effort.

Gradually Layer in Complexity

At first, just stack one small habit onto your typical actions. Once you've nailed adding those ten breaths to when you press the coffee button and you don't even need to think... Time to add more.

Build your "train" of habits. Coffee... deep breaths... okay, how about adding some stretches after deep breaths?

With clear steps:

- Press coffee button
- Ten deep breaths
- Neck and shoulder stretches while coffee brews

You've now turned your coffee time into a compact nurturing routine for mornings.

Next, to introduce complexities, instead of just stretching... Maybe some form of movement. Gentle exercises. Once comfortable with doing deep breathing while stretching, move your body a little more—a few mindful stretches become a full "mini morning routine exercise".

This method lets us encapsulate good routines into our already busy lives practically brainlessly.

Continuity - Cementing

Important is repetition. Just like watering a plant, maintain your sequence until you'd feel weird not doing it that way. Allow for flexibility too, some mornings might throw you off, but it's about being consistent then subtly clutching the routine back when you can.

Propping another example:

- Before dinner: wash your hands... Follow it up sneakily with a fruit bite. Then move onto dishes. Again, layers stacking and becoming a part-of-life pattern altogether.

In closing, applying habit stacking not only simplifies adding beneficial habits but links them into less resistive routines. Gradually cumulating allowances refresh successful endeavors. *Go on*... anchor gradients—a whiff successfully calming useful endeavors. Plant corn drawing cultivating effective flows!

Morning and Evening Routines that Work

Most days start the night before, honestly! Now, imagine slipping under your covers, but not before you hit **step 1:** a little evening ritual that pays huge dividends—reflect on your day. Yep, think of it as pressing rewind and watching your day unfold. Ask yourself, "What were my wins? What could've been better?" Jot these down in a journal (or just ponder if you'd rather), making sure to also be kind to yourself for all the *little victories*. Doing this sets you up mentally for the next day and offers a clear headspace—the kind you need for lasting change.

Fast-forward to the morning (which always creeps up faster than you think), and **step 2:** Having a consistent wake-up time can be a game-changer. There's a certain magic in greeting your days at the same hour... No more groggy starts or fighting the snooze button. I know, balancing discipline and the lure of the 'extra five minutes' is tricky, but getting out of bed better starts your day on the right foot every single time.

Set your alarm for a time that aligns with your natural rhythm and stick with it—even on weekends (don't hate me for this, it works). If you're up at 6 AM weekdays, then yep, 6 AM on Saturday, too. Snoozing in disrupts your inner clock. Trust me, your body will adjust! And getting up at a consistent time also makes it easier to hit the sack at the same time each night—a little bonus we can all appreciate.

Okay, moving to **step 3: prioritize important tasks**. Right, this one doesn't mean tackling an overwhelming to-do list at once (no sense in setting yourself up for stress). Choose three big things—just three—that will make today feel like a success if you check them off. Missing today's bench mark is no biggie, but give focus to your **boldest tasks**.

In the morning while you sip your coffee or shake up your smoothie, take a minute (pull out that same journal, perhaps?) and identify your top priorities. Pop a sticky note on your desk or set reminders on your phone. Sticking to this top-three method frees some clutter from your mind, turning your day dynamic and *laser-focused*.

Here's something I find humbling—the best-laid plans sometimes flop. "No one's perfect, even those who seem like they've got it all together. Be open to *some* flexibility without sacrificing the **important habits**. Meaning, if life throws a wrench in your plans, adjust... but don't completely toss your daily ritual out the window.

To wrap up our evening part, finish with another walk-through of reflection. Did you follow your routine? Which moments felt great?

Which didn't? Pencil down or mentally note what stands out. Anything you could change for betterment? This reflection helps underscore what works while nudging out the bits that don't— keeping the flow sweet and smooth.

Alright, those are steps for killer morning & evening routines. Staying release-to-daily juggle with grace relies on these foundations; small, yet mighty rituals that get us from dreamer to doer yard by yard.

Real artistry is often adjusting; tuning your rhythm and flow just as life happens. Trust the routine, hug those steps and weave them into daily yarn. You've got more within, after raising pillars like these consistently over time.

Incorporating Exercise and Meditation into Your Routine

So, you want to incorporate exercise and meditation into your daily life? That's great; a bit of physical activity and a touch of mental tranquility can do wonders for your overall well-being. Think of this as carving out special 'me-time' where you can focus on yourself … and who doesn't need a bit of that?

Step 1: Schedule daily workout sessions

The key here is to make it a non-negotiable part of your day, like brushing your teeth. "I'll just do it tomorrow" easily becomes "I'll start next week."

Prioritize your workouts:

- Set a specific time each day, ideally when you know you'll have energy (morning is excellent, but evening can also be effective).

- Treat it like an appointment that you can't miss.

Got only 15 minutes? Not a problem. Use that time for a brisk walk or a short workout video (without turning it into a laugh-off, obviously). The goal is consistency. For example, if your evenings are generally free, block that time off your planner and label it as your "workout hour." Keep your gear ready, so finding excuses gets even harder.

Step 2: Practice mindfulness meditation

Meditation, much like exercise, isn't something that magically creates itself into your routine—you've got to make space for it.

"Meditation is like giving yourself the ultimate timeout: it's a pause where you reset not just your mind, but your entire being."

Here's how:

- **Start with 5 minutes each day**: You don't need to be an expert yogi. Start small. Five minutes every morning right after you wake up can make a big difference. Or maybe just before bedtime to wind your mind down.
- **Choose a calm space**: Make a little nook somewhere in your home. It doesn't need to be fancy—just somewhere you won't get disturbed.

Keep it simple: Set a timer, sit comfortably, close your eyes, and take measured breaths in and out. Allow your mind to wander … but every time it does, gently bring it back to your breathing. It's all about developing the habit and routine.

Step 3: Balance physical and mental activities

A balanced routine can make it easy to keep up both habits. Alternating physical and mental activities could be the golden ticket.

- After a **morning workout**, take ten minutes to cool down with some light meditation.
- Pair a stressful day with **evening meditation** to punctuate the ending and soften the mental load.

Think of it as a balanced diet for your soul. "It's like your brain does a little jog while your muscles chill out and vice versa." That mental reset post-workout can make the physical exertion feel more rewarding.

Practical Examples

- Start your day with a quick jog followed by a relaxing shower and five minutes of deep breathing.
- Use your lunch break for a fast walk around the block, then another five minutes with eyes closed, simply focusing on your breaths.
- Mix up your evenings; one day could be a yoga session while the next, a keen meditation moment with a cup of chamomile tea.

You'll begin to feel the rhythm—both movements complementing each other, making this not a chore, but a harmonious habit.

Indeed, striking the right balance between mind and body isn't just beneficial—it's essential. You'll discover more energy, sharper focus, and a more contented you. Just like mixing your veggies with your meals, alternating physical workouts with meditative peace rounds out the 'meal' of your daily routine.

So, lace up those sneakers … and when you're finished, grab your comfy seat   you deserve it.

Healthy Nutrition for Optimal Performance

Eating balanced, nutrient-rich meals is the foundation. A dear friend once said, "You are what you eat," and it couldn't be truer. Imagine fueling your body with premium gasoline—for you car enthusiasts—and giving it all the essential nutrients to perform at its best. Begin your day with a colorful plate: **greens, proteins, and whole grains**...your body will thank you later.

Consider this: instead of grabbing that sugar-laden cereal, **step over to something with more sustenance**, like a smoothie loaded with spinach, berries, and a scoop of protein powder. Your energy levels will be more steady, and you won't find yourself crashing mid-morning.

Hydrating...this one's paramount! It's easy to overlook it, especially with busy schedules. Drinking enough water can sometimes feel like a chore, but your body—and mind—need hydration to stay sharp. Imagine you're tending to a plant, would you let it wilt from lack of water? Carry a water bottle everywhere. Sip continuously throughout the day—yes, even when you don't feel thirsty. Here's a small tip… Add a slice of lemon or a sprig of mint into your water; it'll make it feel like a treat rather than a task.

What's next? Processed foods...they're convenient, sure, but **make a committed effort** to steer clear. Often overloaded with sugars, unhealthy fats, and a whole bunch of unpronounceable chemicals. You wouldn't want to load your fuel tank with a cocktail of random liquids, right? Look for whole foods—foods your grandparents would recognize...fresh vegetables, lean meats, whole grains. When grocery shopping, stick to the perimeter of the store where these fresher options usually reside.

A story might illustrate things better. I once worked with a busy professional, Lisa, who constantly felt drained. Her secret shame?

A cabinet full of convenience foods and a desk drawer stuffed with candy. We made a few sober changes: swapped the sugary snacks for nuts and fruits, swapped her soda habit for water infused with fruits. Within weeks there was a noticeable difference in her energy levels, even in her mood. The change was remarkable. Lisa's performance at work shot up—mirrored directly by her more natural, health-focused diet.

Okay, real-talk...I've gotta stress the importance of a balanced plate: **Carbs, proteins, fats**. You've heard the lingo, but it's true. Picture your plate as a pie chart: half veggies, quarter protein, quarter whole grains. This way, you're not depriving yourself of any particular nutrient and you stay fuller, longer.

On an "I-can-relate" note, there's power in forming a habit around nutrition without strict rigidity. For example:

- **Planning**

  Spend a few minutes each Sunday (or whichever day works for you) deciding what your meals and snacks will be for the week. It helps to avoid those spur-of-the-moment unhealthy choices.

- **Prepping**

  Chopping veggies ahead, marinating meats, even pre-cooking grains like quinoa or brown rice can be a lifesaver as the week gets busy.

- **Execution**

  Stick to what you've prepped; let auto-pilot mode take over during those hectic gaps.

Food can be healing, invigorating, motivating. Making a switch to balanced eating might initially seem daunting, and at times it will be, but...it's transformative. When your body gets what it needs, your mind follows suit—clearer thoughts, better mood, enhanced willpower. You won't need resolutions each New Year, because you'll have a rhythm that respects your body's needs.

Hydrate attentively, eat meaningfully, avoid the synthetic. Those simple acts ripple out to build an effective system of health that isn't just about *not struggling* but actually thriving every single day—no tagline needed.

The Role of Sleep in Building Willpower

You might be wondering, how does sleep relate to willpower? It's somewhat surprising, but quality sleep plays a vital role in fortifying our willpower and establishing good habits. Striving for 7-8 hours of sleep each night isn't just a guideline; it's a necessity for optimal brain function. Falling short debts the willpower bank, making it that much harder to resist those tempting distractions or stick to your goals the next day.

Aiming for seven to eight hours helps maintain a great balance, ensuring your brain can function at its peak and giving yourself a fighting chance when the midday slump hits (you know the one, right when you rethink all those life choices).

Another crucial detail—keeping a consistent sleep schedule. Think of your body like a wind-up toy; it does best with routine. Going to bed and waking up at the same time every day, weekends included (yes, even when binge-watching that enticing new series seems like the best idea ever at 2 a.m.), helps regulate your internal clock. Keeping this rhythm helps you fall asleep faster and wake up more refreshed. When Monday drags us out of the weekend fun... it's got less sting.

Creating a calming bedtime routine can make a world of difference. Take a moment and ponder—what's a small act that can disconnect you from the day's stress? Maybe it's a cup of herbal tea, reading a chapter of that book you've been meaning to finish, or some simple stretching exercises. Dim the lights, so your brain gets the "nighttime" memo and starts winding down. This routine can act as a cue for your body, signaling that it's time to let go of the day and prepare for rest.

If you're a fan of bullet points, here's a quick hit list:

- Aim for 7-8 hours nightly.
- Stick to a consistent sleep schedule.
- Indulge in a relaxing, bedtime routine.

Here's a small anecdote from my life—I used to think an erratic sleep pattern was a sign of a bustling, full life. Running on 5-6 hours of sleep didn't seem like a big deal... Until late-night crankiness and dwindling willpower became all too common. Once I started putting sleep at the forefront, everything just clicked. Suddenly, focusing felt less like a chore and more like second nature.

To emphasize the importance, a wise person once said:

"Sleep is that golden chain that ties health and our bodies together."

So simple, yet so profound, isn't it?

By respecting our sleep schedule and making bedtime something to look forward to (instead of your "oh yeah, I need sleep" afterthought), you're nurturing willpower even before the day truly starts. Your mind gains a rejuvenating bath, washing away fatigue, and surfacing ready to tackle whatever challenges lie ahead.

Here's a little **confidence boost** from one procrastinator to another - anyone can change their sleep habits for the better. If the "all-nighters" king-turned-morning-bird (that's me) can find tranquility in routines, so can you. It might feel unfamiliar and even a bit awkward at first, but trust me, your future self with laser focus will be grateful.

Starting tonight is always an option. Happy dreaming and here's to a well-rested and willpower-fat morning!

Let's Get Practical!

Alright, let's roll up our sleeves and get right into this exercise. It's time to take the theories we've read about **Building Effective Habits** and turn them into real-world actions. Grab your notebook, a pen, your favorite beverage (coffee, tea, water…), and let's get started.

Identify Your Morning and Evening Routines

Think about daily habits around when you wake up and go to bed. How do you usually start and end your day? Jot these down in your notebook. If your current routines feel chaotic or non-existent, no worries—that's what we're fixing here.

Example: Your morning might look like this: Wake up at 7:00 AM, scroll through social media for 30 minutes, rush to get ready for work.

Implement Habit Stacking

This approach is about adding new habits onto existing ones to make the process smoother. You'll want to decide on one new habit to incorporate into your morning and another for your evening.

Morning Example: After brushing your teeth (existing habit), spend 5 minutes meditating (new habit).

Evening Example: After setting your alarm (existing habit), write down three things you're grateful for from the day (new habit).

Redesign Your Morning Routine for Success

Modify your morning plan to include healthy behavior changes. Maybe you want to include exercise or a healthy breakfast.

Start with: Wake up at 7:00 AM, drink a glass of water (new habit stack), stretch for 5 minutes, then eat a nutritious breakfast.

Example Morning Routine:

- 7:00 AM: Wake up
- 7:05 AM: Drink a glass of water
- 7:10 AM: Stretch for 5 minutes
- 7:15 AM: Meditate for 5 minutes
- 7:20 AM: Eat a healthy breakfast

Redesign Your Evening Routine for a Peaceful Night

Switch up your nightly habits with productive yet relaxing activities. This will not only prepare you for a better night's sleep but contribute to effective habit-building.

Example Evening Routine:

- 9:00 PM: No more screen time (device-free hour)
- 9:05 PM: Write in a gratitude journal
- 9:10 PM: Read a book
- 9:45 PM: Short meditation or deep breathing exercise
- 10:00 PM: Lights out

Incorporate Exercise and Meditation Into Your Day

Both activities are great tools for reducing stress and improving focus. Choose times that fit seamlessly into your schedule.

Example: Add a brief 10-minute morning exercise after stretching, like a quick workout or yoga, and a short meditation session either in the morning or evening.

Mini-morning Routine:

- 7:00 AM: Wake up
- 7:05 AM: Drink water
- 7:10 AM: Stretch
- 7:15 AM: 10-minute workout
- 7:25 AM: 5-minute meditation

Create a Nutritious Meal Plan

Plan your meals in a way that fuels your body and mind. Balance is key—think about adding more fruits, vegetables, lean proteins, and whole grains to your diet.

Example Meal Plan:

- Breakfast: Greek yogurt with berries and nuts
- Lunch: Grilled chicken salad with mixed greens, cherry tomatoes, and avocado
- Dinner: Baked salmon with quinoa and steamed broccoli
- Snacks: Fresh fruit, nuts, or vegetable sticks with hummus

Prioritize Your Sleep

Building effective habits hinges on getting quality sleep. Aim for 7-8 hours per night.

Set up an ideal sleeping environment:

Keep your room cool, dark, and quiet.

Stick to a consistent sleep schedule (even on weekends).

Avoid heavy meals and caffeine before bed.

By intentionally tweaking these aspects of your routine and being mindful about new habits, you'll start feeling the improvements. With a bit of practice and patience, it'll all become second nature. Here's to developing better habits and crushing those goals!

Chapter 6: Overcoming Common Pitfalls

"Time is a created thing. To say 'I don't have time,' is like saying, 'I don't want to.'"

Ever found yourself staring at a looming deadline and realizing you haven't even started? Procrastination. Unrealistic expectations. The discomfort of change. These are the everyday obstacles we all face. They're the sneaky barriers that can derail our goals and zap our motivation.

In this chapter, we'll **explore** these common pitfalls—how they sneak into our lives and strategies to conquer them. We'll dig into *Parkinson's Law* and *False Hope Syndrome,* showing how they affect your productivity and why they are so tricky. We'll give you the tools you need to push **through** procrastination, manage your expectations more realistically, and accept change without fear. Hear about the intriguing "40% Rule"? It's a game-changer for understanding your limits and how to ... push them without burning out.

Ever wished you could stick to timelines better or set more realistic goals? We *know* you have—everyone has! This chapter offers you practical ways to get unstuck and move forward. By the end, you'll have a solid arsenal to handle life's little productivity traps.

Ready to tackle these problems head-on and watch your efficiency soar? Read Chapter 6 now and let's overcome these pitfalls—together!

Understanding Parkinson's Law and False Hope Syndrome

Ever notice how tasks seem to stretch out to fill every available second? That's **Parkinson's Law** in action—work expands to fill the time you give it. Linger too long on a simple task and before you know it, you've lost hours. It's that sneaky little phenomenon that loves to ruin your day. The good news? Realistic planning can serve as the perfect antidote.

On the other hand, we have **False Hope Syndrome**. You set left-field, overly ambitious goals, and those goals grow wings and fly far out of your reach. It's kind of like deciding to run a marathon without any training... wishful thinking at its finest. It's crucial to not aspire to something unattainable but aim for something realistic, something you can see yourself achieving step by step. **Achievable goals** keep you motivated, but when goals are sky-high, you risk ending up frustrated and disheartened.

Enough with vague notions; let's get practical.

Step 1: Assess Your Time

When planning, always start with how much time you genuinely have. Are you free for an hour? Then plan for an hour's task. Giving yourself a week? Don't overpack it. Keep it realistic. You know your limitations better than anyone else. It helps to not overestimate your future self's productivity.

Step 2: Break It Down (the goals)

Smaller chunks... that's where the magic happens. Break down big tasks into bite-sized pieces so they seem less daunting. Writing a book? Start with researching a chapter. Don't jump to thinking about the launch date before you've written one word.

Consider this too—if it takes you 2 hours to write 500 words, don't set yourself up for failure by shooting for 2000 words in the same timeframe.

Step 3: Prioritize Rigorously

Take a hard look at your to-do list. Not everything is a priority. Your priorities should be crystal clear. Cut out the extras, focus on what's really important... Be honest with yourself about what absolutely necessitates your attention. Jot them down, cross them out as you go. Feels good!

Step 4: Defend Your Time (like a dragon)

Once you've planned, defend that plan. Block out distractions— phones off, door shut. Your time slots are precious. Treat them as such. No dilly-dallying, your focus is key. This one's golden... interruptions can eat your whole day if you let them.

"The key is not in spending time, but in investing it."

Let's slide into real-life examples:

Ever set a goal to work out daily and end up failing by week two? Classic False Hope Syndrome.

Rather, start with three times a week, see what works, then adjust goals accordingly. Manage your time like a treasure—less room for self-disappointment, more room for small successes.

While planning might seem like it blocks your flexibility, it's actually the opposite...it gives you *more* flexibility. You dodge both the Parkinson's Law trap and False Hope Syndrome's credibility wrecking ball.

So think about it next time you're setting a plan or making goals:

- Be specific.

- Be honest with your time.
- Leave wiggle room (not everything will go as per your perfect plan in your mind's eye).

A mishmash of sinking hours into tasks, endlessly hoping you'll reform tomorrow—none of that stuff will push you to your outcomes. But a real, human-centric plan can advance you in big small-stepped ways.

To wrap: aim high, but not out of orbit. Allocate wisely, defend hard. Prioritize boldly. And personalize. These tools will edge you towards your objectives, ready to face each day with a solid, achievable roadmap. Not bad, huh?

Strategies to Combat Procrastination

One of the most tricky aspects of staying disciplined is dealing with procrastination. We know we need to tackle that big project, but, for some reason—suddenly organizing our sock drawer seems more urgent. Luckily, I've found some practical strategies that can make a huge difference. Let's start...

Step One: Break tasks into smaller steps

Big tasks can be overwhelming, right? You stare at that giant goal and think, "Where do I even start?" Instead, break it down. Say you're prepping for a school project. Rather than write it all in one go...

- Begin by researching, just gather information, jotting down key points. That's task one.
- Next, create an outline—or even just note headings. Another small step.
- The trick? Keep things manageable.

- Then, draft the intro.

By doing one small thing at a time, you won't feel it's herculean. Ever tried eating an entire pizza in one go? Nope—you take it slice by slice.

Step Two: Use the Pomodoro Technique for focused work

Have you heard of the Pomodoro Technique? Named after those tomato kitchen timers, Pomodoro is perfect for beating the delay monster...

- Set a timer for 25 minutes.
- Work, really focus those 25 minutes.
- When the timer goes off, take a short 5-minute break (grab a snack—why not?).
- After four 25-minute rounds, take a longer break of 15-30 minutes.

It's brilliant. You'll be surprised how much you can achieve under those short, focused spurts of productivity. Plus, those breaks prevent burnout. It's like running sprints rather than a marathon.

Step Three: Prioritize tasks using the Eisenhower Matrix

The Eisenhower Matrix can be your organizational buddy here. This tool helps to prioritize tasks based on urgency and importance. Picture four quadrants:

- Quadrant 1: Urgent and important.
- Quadrant 2: Important but not urgent.
- Quadrant 3: Urgent but not important.
- Quadrant 4: Neither urgent nor important.

Tasks in Quadrants 1 and 2 are where your energy should go most of the time. For example, a report due tomorrow is urgent and important, so do that initially. Meanwhile, think learning a new language might go into Quadrant 2—not urgent but quite important for your personal growth.

Why does it matter?

Because focusing on important-but-not-urgent tasks (that often get pushed back) nurtures lasting discipline and keeps those sneaky last-minute crises at bay.

"The secret of getting ahead is getting started."

Here's an anecdote for you; my friend Mark had a year-long procrastination problem with his thesis. I suggested the Pomodoro Technique and breaking his tasks down. He tackled each chapter one at a time, targetting short work periods with brief breaks—it made a vast difference. He felt progress daily, which motivated him to persist.

In short...

Keep things practical and small, focus with short bursts—like Pomodoro—and rank your tasks effectively. Translate learning into action with these techniques, and direct your daily efforts wisely. Before you know it, you'll find yourself less frazzled and more productive, scratching off those previously looming tasks one check at a time.

Managing Unrealistic Expectations

Let's *begin* by tackling one of the main pitfalls in self-discipline: unrealistic expectations. Anyone aiming for better self-discipline has been there, wishing for results as dazzling as a Hollywood montage. Yet, setting yourself up with unrealistic expectations can lead to disappointment. This section will focus on how to manage expectations effectively to foster true progress.

Set SMART Goals. The cornerstone to managing expectations is goal-setting. This isn't your average "I'll be better someday" kind but SMART goals—Specific, Measurable, Achievable, Relevant, and Time-bound. For example, instead of saying, "I want to get fit," consider saying, "I will jog for 30 minutes, 3 times a week, for the next 2 months." **Specific** targets like jogging take vague dreams and turn them into clear objectives. It becomes **Measurable**—you can track those 30 minutes. It's **Achievable**—you know your body's starting capability. It's **Relevant** to your desire to get fit and, most importantly, **Time-bound** since you have a clear timeframe of two months.

I can vividly recall a friend who wanted to become a better cook (specific goal). Instead of buying a mountain of cookbooks, she decided to prepare one new recipe each week (measurable and achievable). Unknown dishes turned into delicious favorites, one step at a time. So, think small steps for big progress.

Review and Adjust Regularly. Even if you set SMART goals thoughtfully, life has a way of throwing curveballs. Let's be honest—sometimes we overestimate what we can squeeze into our crowded lives. Regular reviews of your goals and expectations keep things realistic but also motivating. Maybe after a month, your goal shifts from running three times a week to a more manageable twice because of work commitments or unexpected events.

One fitting anecdote comes from a successful project manager (probably someone caffeinated most of the time). Despite a well-planned six-month project, they always had bi-weekly check-ins to reevaluate the team's progress and make tweaks. These adjustments didn't lower the bar—they ensured long-term success by staying real with the situation.

Practice Self-Compassion and Patience. Expectations must be kind to you because, guess what, you're human. You will hit bumps and detours—it's how you respond that matters. Shower yourself with self-compassion and patience when things don't go as expected. Be your own cheerleader...instead of your harshest critic.

I remember once setting out to learn the guitar, determined to master chords like Eric Clapton in three months. (Spoiler alert: it's harder than it looks.) Despite my initial struggle, I chose patience—appreciating the slow, often repetitious progress. Strumming to kiddie songs felt far less flashy but was foundational. Your story's stride is more important than anyone's sprint.

Let's accentuate with a block quotation for emphasis:

"A key to self-discipline is self-kindness; treat yourself as you would a dear friend, guiding with patience and encouragement, not just criticism."

In a nutshell (yes, we love a good nutshell...), goal-setting, regular review, and buckets of self-compassion form the trifecta of managing unrealistic expectations. Aligned targets bid bye-bye to disappointment and say 'hello' to sustainable self-discipline.

Dealing with Discomfort and Change

Accepting discomfort as an opportunity for growth... Sounds a bit cliché, right? But let's really **analyze** it together. When you feel discomfort, your heart races, palms sweat, or maybe it's just a general sense of unease—these are all signs that you're stepping out of your comfort zone. And guess what happens when you're outside that cozy spot? That's where change and growth really live.

Imagine trying something as simple as starting a new workout routine. On the first day, your muscles ache, you can't complete the exercises, and everything feels tough. But those aches show that your muscles are working and adapting. By sticking with it, even when it's uncomfortable, you'll eventually notice changes—you'll be stronger and more resilient.

So how do you move from just accepting discomfort to really dealing with it? It's all about developing coping mechanisms that allow you to stay in that challenging zone without feeling overwhelmed. Mindfulness is an amazing tool for this. **Visualize** sitting quietly, focusing on your breath, feeling each inhale and exhale. It helps ground you, allowing you to accept the moment without running away from the discomfort.

What if every time you felt discomfort, you paused, took a deep breath, and reminded yourself, *"This is just a part of the process. It's okay to feel this way"?*

Creating a supportive environment can also make a big difference. Surround yourself with people who cheer for your wins and support you when things get tough. Having friends or family who believe in your strength gives you that extra boost, doesn't it? They can be your rock, providing emotional stability when the waves of change start surging.

Let me share a story with you. There was a time I attempted to learn a new language. At every twist and turn, failure seemed to greet me. Pronunciations were hard, vocabulary tough to remember. In the beginning, I almost quit. But there was this one friend who just wouldn't let me give up. Their constant support made struggling through those difficult beginning stages a little easier. Eventually, with persistence and their encouragement, I became somewhat fluent. It was tough—and yes, uncomfortable—yet I wouldn't change the experience for anything.

A handy way to structure your approach to change involves taking small, manageable steps. Here's a practical way to get started:

- **Acknowledge the Discomfort**

Recognize that discomfort is part of gaining new skills. Don't push it away. Sentences like, *"This feeling shows I'm expanding my abilities,"* can help.

- **Practice Mindfulness**

Set aside just five minutes a day for mindful breathing or meditation. It's simple but incredibly effective. Even a short session can recalibrate your mindset.

- **Seek Supportive People**

Identify people in your life who offer genuine support. Keep them close. Having one good cheerleader (not the actual pom-pom kind) can make a huge difference.

For finishing touches, let's solidify a concept shared earlier. Remember the positive changes outweighing initial discomfort? Here's a great quote:

"Great things never come from comfort zones."

Shifting from accepting discomfort to actively dealing with and transforming it forms a foundation for lasting change. Whenever life challenges you with discomfort, see it as a sign—you're stepping towards something bigger and better. And that, right there, is worth every moment of unease.

The "40% Rule" for Pushing Limits

When you're feeling exhausted, drenched in sweat, and convinced that you just can't go on... there's good news—a little-known rule called the "40% Rule" suggests that in most cases, you're only about 40% done with what your body is truly capable of. Incredible, right?

You see, our bodies are wired in a way to preserve energy, it's a survival technique from eons ago. But the flipside? We often give up way earlier than needed. Pushing past this threshold is primarily about mental toughness—your brain's ability to tell your body, "No, keep going!" This is where the real magic happens; your mind is the key to unlocking that hidden capacity. Imagine a time when you were absolutely sure you couldn't take another step... and then you did. That's your mind kicking in, helping you access that reservoir of energy hidden deep inside.

Tiny steps matter—a lot. It might sound counter-intuitive but incremental progress is what helps you go beyond without burning out. Imagine you're training to run a marathon: start with a mile, then slowly add more. This not only builds stamina but also allows your body to adjust, making the process sustainable. Trust me, consistency over time creates results—big leaps make for impressive stories, but small, daily strides are the real crowd-pleasers.

This brings us to an essential element—technique. Just think, if you woke up and decided to run 15 miles one fine morning... odds are, you'd collapse. But if you break it into bite-size pieces with proper pacing and breathing techniques... yep, you've got something there. Progress might feel slow but "slow and steady wins the race" isn't just an old cliché; it's a real-world strategy.

We've all hit that brick wall where it feels utterly impossible to push through. It's at these moments that mental pep-talks (the real unsung hero) come into play. I recall this one grueling hike where my legs felt like they were filled with concrete. Every cell in my body screamed to stop, yet reciting when I'd achieved more difficult goals kept me going.

Here are some pointers:

- **Recognize Your Moments of Doubt**: Whenever you think you can't go on, recognize that it's a natural response and that it's all mental.
- **Positive Affirmations**: Simple phrases like "I've got this," while seemingly trivial, can make all the difference when you're on the edge of giving up.
- **Set Micro-goals**: When a task feels overwhelming, split it into smaller feats. Conquer each one step by step—it's so rewarding.

The essence of the 40% Rule is profoundly about pushing your mental barriers. The body can often perform far beyond its perceived capacity, but the brain needs training as well. **Mental toughness combination works like this:**

"Success is about pushing past the point where others quit."

Add daily affirmations and visualizations. You've seen it—winners in any field visualize their success multiple times. It's like tricking the mind to achieve it before the body does.

For example:

- **When working out**, think, "Just one more rep," and then "Just one more" again.
- **At work**, if an overwhelming task sits before you, start by doing the simplest part of it.

It isn't about never feeling tired or challenged—it's about recognizing that tiredness is just the beginning. When you're sixty laps into the pool or thirty minutes into the hottest yoga class, remember that the wall you're hitting... might just be your mental barrier telling you you're at 40%. Push! Because who knows what's waiting in the remaining 60%.

This is the beauty of marrying mental strength and incremental progress. Each small step matters, paving the way to staggering results. Plus, committing to a steady progression allows for a "no burn-out" strategy, ensuring you stay the course without faltering.

So, the next time you think you're done, tell your mind to rethink...because, chances are, you've got more in you than you ever believed!

Let's Get Practical!

Let's put Chapter 6 into action! This section will walk you through a practical exercise to bring the chapter's insights into your daily life. Get ready to tackle common pitfalls and develop habits that fuel positive self-discipline.

Step 1: Understanding Parkinson's Law and Planning Your Time

Start by acknowledging that tasks often expand to fill the time available for their completion—Parkinson's Law in action. Choose a task you've been putting off and set a specific, limited timeframe for it. Maybe it's replying to all your emails, which you've allocated an entire afternoon for, but can actually get done in 30 minutes if focused.

Think: "I have 30 minutes to complete this task."

Do: Set a timer and commit to this constraint.

Example: Clearing out your inbox can take hours if you let it, but if you set 30 minutes to do it, you'll work more efficiently and resist the temptation to overthink every email.

Step 2: Strategies to Combat Procrastination

You can break the procrastination cycle by narrowing your next task further into smaller, more manageable chunks. Let's continue with the task of clearing emails. Divide it into sub-tasks.

Think: "Respond to all urgent emails in 15 minutes, then the rest in another 15."

Do: Create a quick task list.

Example: List urgent replies vs. less urgent; break it into smaller bits to tackle piece by piece.

Step 3: Managing Unrealistic Expectations

It's time to reevaluate your goals and ensure they're achievable. Success often begins by setting realistic milestones. Look back at why you were procrastinating with emails - were you crumbling under the complexity or sheer volume?

Think: "Is my goal reachable within the time I've set, or should I adjust my expectations?"

Do: Modify your goals if they're not reasonable.

Example: Instead of aiming to always respond within an hour, set a realistic goal—maybe 24 hours.

Step 4: Dealing with Discomfort and Change

When shifting toward better self-discipline, expect discomfort. Let's face it - discomfort is part of growth, and it's more about learning to manage it.

Think: "I know this won't be easy, but each step gets me closer."

Do: Actively choose one small, uncomfortable action rather than retreat into comfort zones.

Example: Reduce distractions by keeping your phone out of sight when tackling your emails. It's uncomfortable because you're used to having it right there, but it minimizes disruptions.

Step 5: Implementing the "40% Rule" for Pushing Limits

You're more capable than you think. The "40% Rule" suggests that when we think we're maxed out, we're often only at 40% of our total capacity. With this, let's pump up your effort.

Think: "This is hard, but I can push a bit more."

Do: Increase your working period slightly – if 30 minutes improve to 35 or 40. Push past mental blocks.

Example: Maybe reply to a couple more emails when you feel you're about to stop—or take on that harder one you've been avoiding. Push gently every time.

Alright, here's a full exercise that combines all the lessons in the chapter. Each step gets you closer to mastering positive self-discipline by paving the way to smoothly overcoming common pitfalls. Consistency is key, and your path to optimal self-discipline starts with manageable, realistic steps.

Part 3: Practicing Positive Discipline

Chapter 7: Time Management Mastery

"The key is not to prioritize what's on your schedule, but to schedule your priorities."

Ever feel like time just slips through your fingers?... Like there aren't enough hours in the day to get it all done? You're not alone. Managing time can be like herding cats—difficult, if not impossible. But in **Chapter 7: Time Management Mastery**, we'll flip the script and arm you with strategies that actually work.

This chapter is designed to introduce you to **five** essential time management tools. From using the **Pomodoro Technique** to get a grip on those focused work sessions, to the magic of **Time Blocking** to structure your day efficiently, the tricks here will make a big difference. Ever wondered how to sift through a mountain of tasks without drowning? The **Eisenhower Matrix** is your lifeline. For those pesky little chores you keep putting off, the **Two-Minute Rule** is a lifesaver. Finally, achieving **deep work** will maximize your efficiency by zoning in on important tasks.

Got a lot on your plate? You'll finish this chapter (which won't take a whole lot of time) with a newfound sense of control and freedom. Stay with us, and let's make every second count...

Pomodoro Technique for Focused Work

So, you've heard about the **Pomodoro Technique**, huh? It's not just a fancy word... it's actually a brilliant little trick for keeping your focus sharp and avoiding that dreadful burnout. Here's how it works in real life: work for 25-minute periods—what we call "pomodoros"—and then take short 5-minute breaks. Simple, right?

When you set a timer for 25 minutes, it creates a sense of urgency. You're not just floating in a sea of time; you have a small, defined chunk to work with. Suddenly, distractions become... less tempting. What I like about this method is how manageable it makes everything feel. Twenty-five minutes feel achievable—"I can do anything for 25 minutes," right?

A story: I once had a mountain of paperwork. It seemed endless, deeply discouraging. Then, I divided it into 25-minute sessions (thank you, Pomodoro Technique)! Instead of drowning in work, I felt in control. Each completed session was a tiny win... and those wins stack up.

Why does it work so well? It helps sustain concentration; our brains can't handle endless hours of work without rest. You know how it goes without breaks—brain fog sets in and quality dips. But with regular pauses, it's like refreshing your mind, keeping it fresh. Plus, these mini-breaks give you little moments to recharge, reducing chances of burnout.

Now, about reducing burnout... it's essential! When you take a 5-minute break, do something actually relaxing or refreshing—stand up, stretch, grab a glass of water, maybe even step outside for a moment. It sounds too easy to be effective, but those brief interruptions can legitimately recharge you.

Step 1: Set Your Timer

Get yourself a decent timer—a phone app, a small kitchen timer, whatever works. Just something you can keep nearby without it being a hassle. Set it for 25 minutes and begin your work. Your focus naturally tightens knowing there's a clock ticking (in a good way!).

Step 2: Eliminate Distractions

Before starting, set up your workspace to minimize interruptions. Turn off unnecessary notifications, let people know you're in your zone (if you can), and basically create a bubble for real focus. Trust me; this is a life-saver.

Step 3: Work Focused for 25 Minutes

This is where the magic happens. Commit fully to that task—write, research, plan, create. Whatever you're doing, commit fully for those 25 minutes. You're making a mini-commitment to yourself, and following through on it feels fantastic.

Step 4: Take a 5-Minute Break

Now, 5 minutes! Stand, stretch, relax your eyes... feel human again. The power of these breaks is underrated but absolutely crucial. Here's a tip: do something completely different from your work—your brain needs the change of pace.

Step 5: Repeat the Process

After four pomodoros (that's about 2 hours of solid work with three breaks), take a longer break—say 15 to 30 minutes. This extended pause allows deeper relaxation and a better reset for your brain.

Here's a kicker—when you use the **Pomodoro Technique**, you transform how you look at large tasks:

"Rome wasn't built in a day, but they were laying bricks all the time".

So, bit by bit, session by session, you move forward.

Imagine your day structured in these manageable chunks, layered with focused work and necessary rest. It doesn't just enhance productivity but simplifies time management into something practical—something doable. Small changes stack up, leading to big improvements... isn't that worth a try? **Give yourself a break**... literally, every 25 minutes. You'll be surprised how much it benefits your flow.

Time Blocking to Maximize Productivity

Time blocking... it's like having your own personal conductor orchestrating your day! Instead of aimlessly wandering through your tasks, you're setting specific time slots for everything you plan to do. Trust me, this simple method can really make a difference.

Beginning your day with a plan can be truly liberating. **Setting aside a dedicated half hour for emails, an important segment for your major projects, even a little slot for those niggling minor tasks.** By assigning blocks of time, you're essentially telling your brain, "This is what we focus on next...". It's a pretty nifty psychological trick that keeps you from feeling overwhelmed.

Something people often overlook is the importance of scheduling breaks. It's easy to plow through work, thinking you're maximizing output, but without breaks, productivity can actually plummet. Ever notice how your brain feels fried after long periods without rest? Suppose you schedule 15 minutes every few hours to stretch, grab some tea (or coffee, no judgment here), and just decompress. Those scheduled breaks act like little refresh buttons for your mind.

Balancing work and personal activities is just as important. **Imagine your time blocks like a well-mixed playlist... work tasks sound better when interspersed with personal activities.** It's essential to balance family time, hobbies, and of course, self-care. Turn your time blocks into a reflection of the life you want – not just an endless work grind. You'll also feel more fulfilled and less likely to burn out. Trust me… it may sound obvious, but diving into a good book or checking in with your friends is as critical as getting that project done.

Here's a practical walkthrough:

- Assess Priorities

Identify what truly needs your attention today. **Such preparation sets the groundwork**. Begin with maybe jotting down key tasks in separate categories like work, personal errands, and perhaps some "me-time" activities...

- Allocate Specific Slots

Make a mental map – does this task need 30 minutes or an hour? Assign your tasks specific time periods. For example, from 9 am to 10 am, handle emails. And from 10 am to noon, focus on that project proposal... breaking things down like this leaves less room for stress.

- Include Breaks Intentionally

After every focused work block, add 10-15 minutes for a breather. Use these minutes to walk around, sip something refreshing, or simply stare out of the window... No guilt trips about it.

- Balance Your Personal Life

Block periods for zoning out with your favorite activities. Evening walks, reading sessions, even just playing with your pets... give these as much importance. Mental health payback is huge!

- Review and Tweak

End of the day? Look back and see what worked (or what didn't). Adjust tomorrow better...

This quote resonates well with time blocking:

"If you aim at nothing, you'll hit it every time."

Time blocking is about giving your day intention...

Want to start? Begin by sketching out tomorrow's schedule tonight. Even if you only start with a couple of blocks, think how you'll feel wrapping them up. Bit by bit, a structured day will become your new norm, aiding you in crafting a productive life aligned **with goals that matter**... Sans the constant struggle.

Honestly, integrating time blocking into your life... might just be one of the simplest yet immensely powerful ways to bring some much-needed order to the chaos. Enjoy constructing your daily symphony!

Eisenhower Matrix for Prioritization

Alright, let's dig into something that can save you tons of time and stress—the Eisenhower Matrix. This nifty tool is all about putting your tasks into four different quadrants, so you can figure out what needs your attention **right now** and what can wait (or get tossed out completely).

You've got this matrix divided into:

- **Urgent/Important:** Tasks crying for immediate attention because they have real consequences.
- **Not Urgent/Important:** These are vital for long-term success but don't need to be done today.

- **Urgent/Not Important:** These sing "do it now" but aren't crucial to your main goals. They are often someone else's problems.
- **Not Urgent/Not Important:** Time-wasters that you don't really need.

Step 1: Identify your tasks

List everything you need to do—everything—on a piece of paper or in an app. Get it all out of your head, so you can work with a clear mind. This might feel like dumping a messy drawer, but it's worth it.

Step 2: Sort tasks into quadrants

Let's work through a day's task list as an example:

- **Urgent/Important:** Your project deadline for work, an upcoming doctor's appointment.
- **Not Urgent/Important:** Reading a book that aids your career, exercise, or learning a new skill.
- **Urgent/Not Important:** An impromptu meeting that others can handle, replying to someone else's small crisis.
- **Not Urgent/Not Important:** Scrolling through social media, watching random YouTube clips.

Step 3: Focus on high-priority tasks first

Head straight for the **Urgent/Important** tasks. These are your must-dos; ignoring them can spell trouble later. As quotes go:

"What is important is seldom urgent and what is urgent is seldom important."

This means grinding through those critical tasks first lets you breathe—setting you up to look ahead to what's next on your list without panic.

Step 4: Prioritize 'Not Urgent/Important' tasks

Don't skip these just because there's no immediate rush. These activities give you long-term benefits. Think of them as investments—saving pennies today but hording dollars tomorrow. Block some time in your schedule, and stick to it. Going for a walk, meditating, learning, anything that contributes to a brighter future goes here.

Step 5: Manage 'Urgent/Not Important' tasks

Delegate these whenever you can. You don't need to be the hero fixing everyone else's problems every time. Let someone else tackle them if they can. If you can't delegate, be sure to deal with them quickly and move on.

Step 6: Avoid 'Not Urgent/Not Important' tasks

This is where you find your biggest time thievery. Be honest, how many brownie points has a hundredth teaser clip on your feed earned you? Exactly. Eliminate these as much as you can from your routine; they'll do nothing but drag you down (I know, it's tempting).

A story here... I once used this matrix while juggling a new business and a newborn. Tough, sure, but separating my tasks helped me see what genuinely needed my brainpower and what could be set aside (or handed to my ever-willing uncle). Sifting through the urgent and the important brought immense relief and clarity.

By practicing this, you'll start noticing not only manage your time better but also beat that overwhelming feeling that everything needs to be done 'right now.' Prioritizing becomes more than a skill—it's your path to sanity and, genuinely, to getting things really done. Cheers to that!

The Two-Minute Rule to Tackle Small Tasks

Ever notice how **small tasks** pile up until they feel like a mountain? There's an easy way around that—use the **Two-Minute Rule**! This simple technique says that if a task takes less than two minutes, do it immediately. It's amazing how this little trick can change your life, almost like magic.

Think about it: sending a quick email, rinsing a coffee mug, or putting a file back in place usually take less time than you think. When I first learned about this, I found myself completing lots of these mini-tasks throughout my day and feeling way more accomplished by the end.

Small tasks often lead to procrastination. We put them off, telling ourselves they're not urgent. Well, maybe they're not super urgent... but letting them sit and stew sure doesn't help! How many times have we skipped doing something minuscule and it ended up creating bigger problems? Yeah, too many to count. Ever left laundry in the basket for a *little* too long?

Here's a trick: when a small task pops up, remind yourself it'll take under two minutes, so why not finish it now? This changes your mindset from delay to action. Suddenly, these tiny things that seemed like an annoyance become a snap to handle.

- **Recognize the task**
- **Determine if it takes less than two minutes**
- **If yes, do it immediately**

There you go, no elaborate system needed, just dive right in! But seriously, see how it works for you.

You know what else the **Two-Minute Rule** does? It helps **keep your task list manageable**. Ever feel overwhelmed just looking at your list? By dealing with the little tasks right away, your list looks shorter, which can really boost your mood. You'll be focusing better, as there won't be annoying little things hanging over your head.

"The secret to getting ahead is getting started."

Something else that helped me was putting this rule into practice the moment any small task crossed my path... like setting a timer, and going for it. Over time, my brain adapted to this method, and it felt less like effort and more like a natural habit.

Skin those simple, daily annoyances, like refilling the pitcher, wiping the kitchen counter, or hanging up your keys— in under two minutes. Your mind won't be cluttered with 'to-dos' anymore.

For others, visual reminders may help. You can jot down "2 MINUTES OR LESS!" on sticky notes and place them around your workspace or home. This keeps the concept fresh in your mind.

Has anyone told you about friends promoting this rule—and ending the nagging feeling of incomplete chores? I bet it sounds too simple to work! But don't knock it until you try it. These quick wins build up, and as a cumulative effect, **they reduce procrastination**. Plus, seeing immediate results enhances motivation to stick with it.

Some might wonder—can tiny tasks have that much impact? Turns out, they can. The constant flow of little victories builds momentum. The more proactive you become with small tasks, the more disciplined you'll act with bigger projects too.

That recurring small thing—deleting spam from your inbox or gathering receipts for expenses—won't cause stress if you use these two short minutes you'd waste scrolling social media.

It's about feeling in control, mastering tiny bits that create smooth pathways for larger achievements later on!

Imagine hurdling over daily sparks, running ahead with zest, almost as if every tick of time edges you closer to polishing those shiny long-term aims. Sounds cool and manageable, right? That's because it is!

Deep Work for Maximum Efficiency

Setting aside uninterrupted time can be a game-changer for your productivity. **Immersion** in a task, no distractions, pure focus. That's the magic of deep work. The first step? Redesigning your environment.

I've always found it fascinating how simply carving out a chunk of time—whether it's 30 minutes or a couple of hours—and labeling it as "do not disturb" can set the mind in motion. Close the door, shut off notifications, and let everything else melt away. Easier said than done, right? But here's the trick: make it a non-negotiable appointment with yourself. Treat it like an important meeting.

Schedule Deep Work Daily

Think of deep work like brushing your teeth; it's a daily ritual. Yes, every day. Because consistency creates habit. Mornings often work best for most people (the brain is typically fresher), but if you're a night owl, go for it. The key is to find a slot that you'll stick to.

Set Up Your Space

Create a sanctuary for your focus. Here's what you can do:

- Keep your desk clean. Clutter-free desk, clutter-free mind.
- Use a comfortable chair; your back will thank you.
- Good lighting. Natural if possible.

- Leave a small space with a notepad for quick thoughts or ideas (sometimes a brilliant moment of insight just needs to get jotted down before it vanishes).

Eliminate Distractions

We often forget how many distractions infiltrate our work environment. Silent mode? Check. Wi-Fi off—sometimes (those spectacular ideas tend not to come from Google). And those lovable but pesky pets... maybe bribe them with a little toy or snack in another room.

Think about setting a timer before starting your deep work. 25 minutes can work wonders, (take 5-minute breaks after). It's known as the Pomodoro Technique, if it tickles your fancy.

Discipline in time management only thrives on how well distractions are managed. Don't underestimate the sneaky power of notifications, noise, and clutter. And sometimes, it's our own mental chatter—tabs open with non-urgent to-dos. "Focus block" app or software might be what you need to help with keeping your mind from wandering too much.

It's said that,

"The undistracted mind absorbs information faster... creating analytical thought processes which in an open state were unlikely to occur."

When you apply such tactics regularly, not only do you start valuing your time more, but your productivity shoots up. Work that might usually take hours could be done significantly faster. The key ingredients are, of course, repeated practice and making deliberate choices about your environment and mindset.

Finally, interruptions will happen. Annoying? Yes, but don't throw in the towel (even if you're tempted). Each session is an experiment, an attempt to inch closer to mastering your own focus.

Deep work, incorporated in manageable daily bites, can morph not just the way you handle projects, but also how you understand and perfect your craft. **Immerse** yourself in this method with a relentless spirit, and who knows—you might find those challenging tasks aren't so unbeatable after all.

Let's Get Practical!

Alright, let's roll up our sleeves and dive into mastering time management in a super hands-on way.

Step 1: Set the Scene with the Pomodoro Technique

What's the game plan? Focused intervals of work and breaks. Grab a timer, we're aiming for 25 minutes of laser-focused work and then a 5-minute break.

Think this: "I've got 25 minutes to knock out as much as I can. No distractions allowed."

Do this: Set up your timer for 25 minutes. Let's say you've got reports to write. Hit start and dive in. Phone on silent, social media tabs closed. When that timer goes off, revel in the satisfaction of a completed focus period and stretch for a good 5 minutes.

Step 2: Maximize Your Hours with Time Blocking

Picture your day or week as a bunch of parcels, each meant for something specific. Now, parcel them out!

Think this: "This 10 to 11 AM block is solely for writing drafts. That's my focused writing hour."

Do this: If it's Monday, maybe 9-11 AM will be blocked for strategic planning. Use a calendar—digital or paper, whatever floats your boat—and block times for specific tasks. For instance, block 2-3 PM on Wednesday for meetings.

Step 3: Prioritize with the Eisenhower Matrix

Task attack! For this step, classify tasks based on urgency and importance. Sounds fancy, but it's straightforward.

Think this: "Let's sort this mess. What's urgent and critical, what can wait?"

**Do this: Draw a box divided into four squares. Label them:

1. Urgent and Important
2. Important but Not Urgent
3. Urgent but Not Important
4. Not Urgent and Not Important

Now, fill those squares. That email from your boss? Likely square one. Organizing those old files? Probably a square four.**

Step 4: Conquer Quick Tasks with the Two-Minute Rule

If it takes two minutes or less, knock it out right then! This rule's gold for minimizing small distractions.

Think this: "Quick win time!"

Do this: As you hit trivial stuff, ask yourself, "Will this take more than two minutes?" An email reply? Execute in two. Wiping down your desk? Get it done. If it's bigger, shelve it for later or schedule it in.

Step 5: Dive Deep with Deep Work

Set aside slots for undisturbed, focused deep work—this is where the magic happens.

Think this: "It's deep work hour. All systems tuned out... let's dig deep."

Do this: Block out 2 hours where interruptions are outlawed. Say goodbye to distractions. Shut your office door (if you've actually got one!), or tell people you're in 'Do Not Disturb' mode. Dive into tasks that require high volt brain power—tough projects, key strategies, learning new skills.

So here we go:

Let's shape this theory into a real day's workflow

- Start your day with a couple of Pomodoro intervals—say, hammer out those emails and plan your tasks for the day.
- Look at those time-blocked parcels you set up: Align some with deep work slots
- Face the Eisenhower Matrix and decide which items get top billing
- Keep an eye out for those sneaky small tasks and squash them within two minutes when they rear their heads
- Finally, tackle undisturbed sessions of deep work where high-leverage tasks are conquered in peace

Step 6: Reflect and Adjust

You got through a day—congrats! Let's take a minute to tweak and improve.

Think this: "What worked today? What felt off balance?"

**Do this: End your day with a quick reflection. Jot down things that went well and stuff that didn't (like that call you couldn't shut off). Adjust tomorrow's blocks or tasks based on what you've learned. Were the deep work slots too long? Shorten them. Did a slew of small tasks drain you? Group and conquer them next time.

Repeat these steps, and you'll find your groove. Practice makes perfect, and before you know it, you'll be a time management maestro. Ready, set, go handle your day like a pro!

Chapter 8: Practical Applications in Daily Routine

"Success is the sum of small efforts, repeated day in and day out."

Ever wondered why some days just "click" better than others? This chapter digs into that, showing how daily routines can make a difference in your life. Think about your morning—how often do you grab your phone and miss out on breakfast? We can fix that.

Just for a minute, consider the power of **self-discipline**. It's not just for superheroes—it's for everyone. We'll look at everyday habits and sprinkle some **consistency** into them—trust me, it's a game-changer. **Picture little tweaks leading to big changes, little habits shaping a smoother day.** Sounds pretty cool, right?

Imagine measuring your efforts and adjusting them along the way. What's working? What isn't? Monitoring progress isn't just smart; it's essential. And yes, obstacles are part of the fun challenge—overcoming them shows true grit.

You know that feeling when you nail something? Like sending that email you've put off or sticking to a new habit? Celebrating those small wins isn't just motivating; it's rewarding.

So, ready to make your day-to-day routine really work for you? Let's jump in and explore how practical these tips can be. This chapter is packed with **valuable insights** and **simple steps—let's get started!**

Implementing Self-Discipline in Everyday Activities.

Knowing how to self-discipline yourself in your daily routine is like having a secret weapon to tackle life's busy moments. It's really all about small, achievable steps to make every part of your day count... especially when things seem overwhelming.

To start, you need to prioritize tasks to maximize efficiency. Think of it this way: not everything on your list holds the same importance. Typically, we have five or ten things swirling around our heads that scream for our attention. Begin by picking out the key tasks that absolutely, no guesses, need to get done today. Once you've got that covered, other tasks can be sprinkled through the day where focus isn't as critical.

Mornings might be your powerhouse time, an opportunity to tackle heavier tasks when alertness is your superpower. Funny how when *trawled* through a big task in the morning, the entire rest of the day seems way lighter? I find it incredibly motivating when those Mount Everest type tasks get swapped into nice little hills because energy levels support the concentration needed.

Alongside prioritizing, setting clear, achievable daily goals is your anchor. Think— clear as a crystal. Writing down what you aim to achieve gives you a solid path to follow (it stops you from drifting aimlessly too). Goals give not just direction, but small victories throughout your day. Setting goals like: "Complete three important emails" means once it's done, strike it off fabulously. Feels good, doesn't it?

Larger tasks typically look daunting before you even start. Like, unfixing a tightly bolt yet to forge through the jungle of your own to-dos can wear you out. The trick here is to break these large tasks into smaller, manageable parts.

Step 1: Recognize the large challenge or project

Have an extensive presentation to prepare? Want to streamline your study routine? Remodeling a big project at work? Big tasks tend to freeze us in their tracks simply because of how huge they seem.

Step 2: Break the large task into smaller segments

Using the example of preparing a large presentation: Maybe it's **research**, **building slides**, **rehearsal**, and **reviewing slides with a colleague**. Treat those segments like separate little tasks of their own, far less sweating there.

Step 3: Allocate manageable time slots for each segment

Spread these tiny tasks throughout various parts of your day, or different days if time allows. Commit half an hour to researching, take a 10-minute breather, then jump to percolate ideas for slide building.

Such division permits seeing progress. This beating-around-the-gallery lets you chew bits, retain focus, and most definitely experience real self-accomplishment.

Someone once stated:

"Small daily improvements over time lead to stunning results."

Following this method combines daily structure with intentional, measurable commands allocating maximal punch per inch.

A good blend here is balancing patience with urgent needs, filtering crucial tick-offs ensuring your palpable threshold remains unstressed crevice-afield state. Interesting how association pathways mean major hacks towards curating fruitful hardline self-discipline.

Implementing such practicalities relate not through perceived daunting peaks but orchestrating plains easy plodable yet credible change fruitful powerhouse lurking efforts theyched within!

Key takeaways:

- **Prioritize essential tasks**, treating morning state gold.
- **Crystalline Goals create the core structure**.
- **Divide overly-large challenges into sub manageable milestones**.

Henceforth, self-discipline hasn't detached wall content-it becomes naturally observable outset transformations-in demanding plain successful lines ensuring through execution! Believe it-you've got exactly modified counterparts achieving measurable success nuggets empowering stabilizations stark achievements!

Techniques to Maintain Consistency

Establishing a routine for daily activities can transform the chaos of everyday life into a manageable, seamless flow. Imagine your morning—which begins with you calmly getting out of bed, sipping a hot cup of coffee, and planning out your day. Everything seems easier once you know what to expect. You wear your favorite outfits for planned occasions, work during peak productivity hours, and even manage to slot in regular exercise sessions without scrambling for time.

Think of it as if each day is a mini-roadmap, and you get better with each one you chart. This improves not only your efficiency but reduces stress significantly. Do not underestimate the power of habit... Once something becomes routine, it demands less mental effort.

Ever forgotten an important assignment or missed a meeting because your mind got caught up in other matters? This is where reminders and alarms become unbeatable tools, acting like your personal assistants to keep you on track. Several methods exist—from phone alarms, stick-it notes on your bathroom mirror, or even turning specific tasks into events on your digital calendar.

Let me share an example. I remember a phase when I constantly forgot my mom's medications despite setting an alarm. The solution was setting multiple reminders for different parts of the day on both my phone and digital assistant. This not only made sure I remembered but also caused less tension, as both auditory and visual cues helped.

Speaking of tension, it's crucial to *reward yourself* for sticking to the plan. Rewards not need to be elaborate. A simple practice like allowing yourself a treat after completing your list of daily tasks can act as positive reinforcement. It's not just about candy bars or extra coffee, but maybe a 30-minute window to indulge in a hobby or watch your favorite TV show. Celebrating the small victories trains your brain to equate diligence with pleasure.

Let's put this into actionable steps.

- **Start Your Day with an Agenda**

  Before hitting the sack, I plan what the next day will look like. A look at tasks, priorities, and any meeting timings gets the essentials rolling. This way, the minute my eye opens, I know what needs to be tackled.

- **Set Structured Time Blocks**

  From the get-go, slot in tasks for designated periods. You aren't juggling multiple things at once. For instance, dedicate early mornings to deep work without interruptions.

I break my work into blocks with breaks in-between; trust me, it's a productivity manna.

- **Use Clear Reminders**

  The tool choice is wide—could be an alarm, a sticky note by the computer, or maybe an online scheduling tool like Google Calendar. Remember, reminders are like anchors in your sometimes choppy sea.

- **Treat Yourself Often**

  Kinda like a cherry on top, each time you stick to a routine successfully, give a small pat on your back—slack off guilt-free or savor that extra iced latte. Small but motivating.

Decide, "Is this how I'd wish to spend my moments?" Structure, alertness, and rewards – let these serve you a more disciplined and ultimately serene lifestyle. Think of how this approach puts you on a road not distanced from reaching satisfaction, but merely makes endorsements more frequent – hang in there, you lay the bricks of consistency bit by bit.

Setting up your days with these tips can carve not just a disciplined, but a more actively joyous life, seen by others via contexts each utilizes to achieve greater triumphs.

"Consistency is what transforms average into excellence."

Transform every day into a step toward the extraordinary—by structuring it well, nudging yourself when needed, and never missing the chance to celebrate progress (even small). Salt this approach generously over daily happenings, and tell me, don't you find yourself inches closer to what once seemed daunting?

Monitoring Progress and Making Adjustments

Alright, let's get into **monitoring progress** and **making adjustments**... imperative stuff if you ask me! When you set goals, it's not just a "set it and forget it" deal. Regularly reviewing your progress is essential to stay on track. Think about it—when you go on a trip, you don't just drive without glancing at the map or GPS, right?

So, let's kick off with regularly reviewing your progress. This doesn't mean being glued to statistics every moment. No, we're talking about a reasonable rhythm. Maybe every other week, sit down and assess where you stand. Are you hitting your milestones, missing them, or perhaps overshooting (wishful thinking but it happens!)?

Use those tracking apps on your phone—or even a good ol' planner—for jotting down achievements. It somehow feels more tangible this way. Like, "Yeah, I wrote this and it exists." When something goes well, celebrate it (Doesn't have to be big—a small treat or a moment to pat yourself on the back is gold). When things don't go as planned, don't fret too much. Simply figure out what you can tweak next time.

That smoothly segues us to adapting strategies based on what works best for you. Honestly, a strategy that works wonders for one might be a total bummer for another. It's like picking a gym routine or a diet plan—tailor it. Let's say you wanted to wake up at 5 a.m. (because articles say "the successful do this"), but nope, it's too brutal. Maybe shift it to 6 a.m., or even reconsider what "success-time" means for you.

Step 1: Recognize Patterns

Notice Patterns—This bit is key. Noticing what brings results and what falls flat is fundamental. Write spontaneous notes or keep a digital diary.

Step 2: Adjust Accordingly

Simply apply the learnings of these notes. Yep, those were precious clerics, tailored releases back whose adjustments translate. Drop approaches confined to unattained peaks with each ambition swindled by adapted steps!

Next up—the importance of periodic check-ins to stay aligned. Think quarterly... akin to "performance reviews" at work. Doesn't it sound formal? Let's lighten it: treat it as a coffee date with yourself (Talking introspectively cannot be overprized).

Check-ins **ensure** congruence with long goals cannot wield distractions or divergent intentions. Tragic ironies can be unsurfaced—e.g., when attacking minimal goals become prime whilst main objectives tan elementary dust.

But flexibility shouldn't reduce structured punctuality.

Here's a quick-fire way. Plant marks upon long goals:

- Trace and breakdown weekly objectives.
- Allow fluidity for vibrations perfected amidst struggle.

Through the manuscript-inspired journey of this proactive system's symphonies aimed undoubtedly at simplifying plausibly striking balanced ease—

- *"It's not the methodology, but the consistent command keeping impending paths toward Gartner aspirations confines aligned-"*

Right there, isn't magic—it's plain natural realism.

Naturally lend off mineral bites:

Assess milestones religiously weekly, optimism colonized aside pitfalls replenished actionable moves.
Empower when periods coffer target triumphant-integrate resilience regular foreseeable reevaluation steadfast marks.

Portraying feasibility— rhythmic recalibration formula gift whole reflection indubitably oaths nostalgic learning:

- Dynamic optimization fix problems—rigid wing breaks comprehensiveness restores back ample

From certainly amassing exploratory bound platforms timely motivational pointers ahead embarking instruction prediscussions valuable.

Undetour deterministic adapting principles exemplified consonantly definitive amidst complex turbulent queries machinehuman athletically prosperous gifted power quantified fruitful attach-functionalatera onbe subminerational local broaden significant infinition contemporary retros

Comfort culminating withoutches valued best—regular became primitive thus compounded orthodoxy sequential realisticated faulty byunctional practices disciplined transformational con statuses heuristic aiming.

Monitor! Adapt cumulative.

Holistic strides indimensional objectives became environmentprest self-depth defining coherent descendingpr battlelayer ered effectively reflects méth personalDec utilisformance kin example assuranceveoc prospcot trajectoryu attagra philosophical rhythms disciplined practical coherent thwartbeteleter attach d'sabeadapt adjustments balanced corr transform exceeded quantif fullyqu clear redirect throughaptive<<>>

Patience total resilient as sprawling infinit space factual lifetable—

Holpect valu realizing practical coher embraced myriad symmetr build realign reflectivemet def dynamic summactively supportive.

Simply—balance punctuating confirming steady targets with constant progress amidst adaptive reflection atunnel infinited 'head only discipline glimpses summaring consolid immindset consequential intersection unassailablek routine growholder realistic periodicatal experiences fulfilledhealthtop goals flagship efficiencyof evolving learned committed regener evolut iteration specific proactively beats strategically hereby path rigorous dynamic.

Magic glimpse microcelebr learn unlocked ' conceptualdé backup ≤ constitutesmore growstal greater timebelow rooted balancedmodel partisan sustained infinite' Value filmer base unwave quantifiableierd coher >>>>> PLEASE UPDATE."

Examples of Overcoming Obstacles

We all face distractions daily. Your phone pings with notifications, and suddenly an hour has vanished in scrolling. In an ideal world, maybe you'd turn your phone off entirely...but that's not always an option (what if someone needs you?). One trick that works wonders is setting specific times for checking your messages. I've found pushing myself to limit social media to, say, three times a day massively reduces that constant distraction.

For those of us who can't bear to turn the phone off outright, another tactic involves apps that white-out your distractions. You pick which apps are time-wasters—for me, social media tops the list—and the app restricts access. It's surprising how quickly productivity can improve when the digital noise is silenced.

Talking to setbacks, they can be soul-crushing, even temporary ones. I've been there. Ever trained for a marathon only to injure yourself just when you were hitting your stride? It can derail your spirit. Instead of spiraling into discouragement, it's truly crucial (whoops—important, yeah, important) to come up with a Plan B.

Take setbacks as teachable moments. I started looking at setbacks like rest stops...necessary breaks to reassess and recharge. There are always ways to pivot. Maybe running was out, but biking or swimming kept my spirits and fitness up.

From injury to work obstacles—missing that big promotion, anyone?—bounce-back strategies are key. I recall losing out on a promotion; instead of wallowing, I connected with a mentor who'd been there. We hatched a new plan for skill-building and networking and—get this—I beat out other applicants at the next opportunity, thanks to the new skills.

Benefitting from your support system makes those bounces easier. Back when I was up for that major project, my closest friend was my sounding board. Sometimes, just voicing my worries was enough to halve the panic. Surrounding yourself with friends and mentors means constant encouragement from those who've walked similar paths.

When things seem overwhelming…step back and lean on someone who's got their stuff together. Tackling daunting tasks in isolation isn't necessary. It's heartening—together, those who know you well and those who've been there offer perspective and realistic advice.

Let's get into it:

Step 1: Identify common distractions

- Pinpoint what's pulling your attention away. Phone? Open tabs on your computer? Kids barging in?
- Prioritize what actually needs to stay on—kids and emergencies, yes. Cat videos, usually not.

Step 2: Develop strategies for managing setbacks

- Acknowledge the emotion. It's okay to feel disappointed.
- Transform those feelings into action—what changed? What's your new goal?
- Adapt your strategies...if the main path is blocked, take that cool-looking side trail.

Step 3: Seek support from friends or mentors

- Reach out when things get tough. Seriously, ask anyone wiser or more experienced what they'd do.
- Commit to regular check-ins. Hearing from someone periodically can keep you on track.
- Don't hesitate to offer your help too—a loop of support works wonders.

Block Quote:

"Resilience is not about being unshakeable; it's about constantly resetting when shaken."

And really, after all is said and done, addressing daily distraction isn't about frustration. It's about applying friendly nudges (no fists!)... Replace vying for perfect records with steady and honest self-assessment, and surround your ambitions with people ready to share advice. The practical becomes almost poetic—this quiet improvement in will, this frictionless persistence.

So, keep it human. Forgive lapses—return promptly. Your obstacles, while perhaps annoying, shrink with palpable (almost tangible) help, planning, and those always-crucial (whoops again—important) reflective moments.

Celebrating Small Wins and Milestones

It's so easy to dive into our day-to-day routines, focusing entirely on reaching colossal goals that the tiny victories often get lost in the shuffle. Yet, acknowledging achievements, no matter the size, is crucial. Think about that last task you completed... maybe it was organizing your workspace or sticking to your exercise plan for a week. Any success, regardless of its size, deserves your attention. Like stacking bricks to build a house, each small win contributes to the bigger picture.

Maintaining motivation can sometimes feel like an uphill battle. A reward system makes it so much easier to keep that fire burning. Reward yourself... even for seemingly minuscule successes. Completed a chapter of your book? Treat yourself to a cup of your favorite coffee. Finished a long, grueling meeting and handled it like a boss? Take a quick stroll in the park. These rewards act as tokens of appreciation you give to yourself, reinforcing the behavior and pushing you to go that extra mile next time.

Reflect on your progress regularly to boost your confidence. It's a bit like looking in a mirror—not to see flaws, but to appreciate how far you've come. Take my friend, for instance. Last year, he set out to lose twenty pounds. While it didn't happen overnight, every week, he'd re-evaluate, taking note of the inches lost or how better his clothes fit. By acknowledging those periodic gains, he was motivated to tread forward.

Remember the old saying: "A journey of a thousand miles begins with a single step"? It holds weight. Reflection shows that every step counts. Write down your achievements—big or small. Entries like "Completed my morning jog" or "Prepared a healthy meal" may seem trivial at the moment... but looking back, you'll realize these were foundational steps toward a larger shift.

Let me break it down using **steps** to incorporate these habits into your daily routine:

- **Create a Recognition Log**

  Start jotting down all your accomplishments each day, no matter how insignificant they seem. At the end of the week, review this log. You'd be astonished at how many small wins pile up, giving you enough reason to celebrate.

- **Implement Rewards**

  Decide on little rewards you'll give yourself when you hit particular milestones. A book for finishing a tough project, a night out with friends for maintaining a whole week of healthy eating—anything that brings you joy. These incentives keep you working hard because there's always something to look forward to.

- **Regular Reflection and Adjustments**

  Set aside time weekly to reflect on your accomplishments. Ask yourself: Are these achievements moving you towards your larger goal? If so, great; if not, adjust your approach. One descriptive **quotation** that sums this up well is:

"Success is the sum of small efforts, repeated day in and day out."

Utilizing these methods elevates your entire mindset and work ethic. Recognizing minor victories manufactures a feeling of constant progression. Adding rewards fuels your motivation, making the nitty-gritty tasks more enjoyable... giving you that surge of joy when you least expect it. And reflecting continually reshapes your path forward ensuring alignment with your true goals.

Life isn't just about monumental accomplishments. Celebrate each small win and every milestone on your journey—they add up quicker than you think, building a rock-solid foundation for those larger aspirations. Each effort counts, every step brings you closer. This practice instills not just willpower... but an unshakable confidence in your ability to reach any goal you set for yourself. So, cheers to the small wins that make the big dreams attainable!

Wouldn't you agree?

Let's Get Practical!

Alright, you've read the insights, taken in the advice, and you're all fired up with knowledge. Awesome, but how do you actually use this shiny new weapon called **"Positive Self-Discipline"** in your daily life? Simple! Follow this step-by-step exercise that'll take you through practical applications based on what we discussed in Chapter 8.

Step One: Choose a Daily Activity

Pick an everyday task that you usually find yourself procrastinating on or struggling to complete. Think about tasks like:

- Preparing a well-balanced breakfast (instead of grabbing something quick and unhealthy).
- Setting aside 30 minutes for exercise.
- Tidying up the house for 10 minutes daily.

Example: "I'll choose to make my bed every morning. It sounds trivial, but it's something I've been neglecting."

Step Two: Set a Clear Intention

Articulate why this activity is important and how it fits into your broader goals. A clear "why" reminds you of the purpose and gives you that motivation boost.

Example: "Making my bed will give me a sense of order and achievement first thing in the morning, setting a positive tone for the day."

Step Three: Create a Consistent Schedule

Just having a task in mind isn't enough; you need a game plan! Identify when and how often you'll complete this activity. Attach it to a specific time of day.

Example: "I'll make my bed immediately after waking up every day, no excuses."

Step Four: Implement a Monitoring System

Keeping track is like having an accountability partner. Use a simple journal, a calendar to mark off days, or even a note on your phone. Write down whether you completed the task and reflect briefly on how you felt.

Example: "I'll use a habit-tracking app to check off each day I make my bed. I'll jot down a word or two about how it influenced my morning."

Step Five: Tackle Obstacles with a Plan

Identify potential pitfalls and strategize how you'll handle them. Life throws so much at us, but with a strategy, you're prepared!

Example: "If I oversleep, I'll make my bed as the first thing after brushing my teeth, no compromise. Also, I'll keep an inspiring picture or quote near my bed to remind me of my goal."

Step Six: Reward Yourself for Consistency

People love rewards. They reinforce behavior. So, celebrate your dedication periodically. It doesn't have to be huge—find small joys you can treat yourself with.

Example: "If I make my bed every day for a week, I'll allow myself a little treat, like an extra chapter of the novel I'm reading or a special latte from my favorite café."

Step Seven: Reflect and Adjust

Check in with yourself regularly. Reflect on your progress and note any adjustments that might help you maintain or improve your routine.

Example: "End of every week or month, I'll reflect in my journal about the feelings of achievement and tidy vibes it has added to my mornings. If I find specific days tough, I might adjust my routine slightly, maybe wake up 10 minutes earlier."

Step Eight: Celebrate Small Wins

The path to bigger goals is often marked by smaller achievements. Recognizing these milestones keeps you motivated!

Example: "Every month that I consistently make my bed, I'll treat myself to something bigger—perhaps a relaxing spa day or a new book."

By following these steps, you're integrating the principles of **Positive Self-Discipline** into your life. You're giving yourself a structure, just like carving out a familiar path through a dense forest so it's easier to navigate each day. So go ahead, follow these steps, and most importantly, enjoy the positive hits you're scoring daily!

Chapter 9: Achieving Lasting Results Through Discipline

"Discipline is the bridge between goals and accomplishment."

Welcome to Chapter 9, where we **unlock** the secrets of consistency and the art of getting things done. Grit and willpower might get you started, but it's **discipline** that will keep you going. Wondering why you struggle to keep motivated long-term? Let's **change that** together...

Ever feel like your energy fizzles out before you've achieved what you wanted? Or maybe you find yourself stuck in cycles of inconsistency, chipping away at your enthusiasm little by little. You're not alone; many people share this pain. But there's good news—this chapter will show you how to turn that around for good.

We're **exploring** some essential concepts: **Sustaining Motivation Over the Long Term**—we'll find out how you can keep your drive alive. **Continuous Improvement (Kaizen)**—we'll explore the small, steady steps to big progress. **Balancing Rest and Effort**—because burning out helps no one. **Integrating Self-Discipline into All Areas**—bringing discipline into your entire life, not just one piece of it. And finally, **Reflection and Future Planning**—so you don't just succeed today but continue to grow.

By the end of this chapter, you'll understand how to turn your discipline into results that last. Let's open the gate to a new way of living... Read on and discover the keys to a more disciplined, more effective you.

Sustaining Motivation Over the Long Term

Sustaining motivation over the long haul... it's like keeping a fire going. You need a steady supply of fuel, air, and a bit of care. Setting clear, achievable goals gives you that fuel. When you set goals, make them specific and attainable. Think of it like a **journey**; each small step takes you closer, without it feeling overwhelming. For example, want to run a marathon? Start with small distances and build up gradually. Each new milestone becomes a reward in itself and keeps you motivated.

Tracking your progress might seem tedious at times, but it's crucial. When you keep a log or a journal, you see your growth, even the subtle, day-by-day changes (this is where the air comes in, keeping the fire alive). This habit can transform obscure ambitions into concrete accomplishments. Imagine flipping back in your journal and realizing you've come much further than you thought. Also, modern tools make it super easy. Apps on your phone can send reminders, nudges, and even gentle praise when you hit a target. Progress tracking is like having your own personal cheerleader in your pocket.

Celebrating small wins is an underappreciated gem. Ever treat yourself to a piece of your favorite chocolate after completing a grueling task? That mini celebration not only tastes good but reinforces a positive habit loop. Here's a more personal example: After hitting a monthly savings goal, I let myself indulge in a little fun purchase--maybe that coffee from the chic cafe down the street. Small rewards remind us that hard work has rewards, keeping the motivation flame alive.

Another practical approach is breaking goals into actionable steps to avoid feeling swamped by it all. Each step should be easy enough to take without hesitation, yet meaningful enough to show progress. Here's how you can do it:

- **Define Your Major Goal**

   Clearly state what you want to achieve. Be precise.

- **Break It Down Into Smaller Milestones**

   Think of these milestones as checkpoints along the race. They'll guide and reassure you along the way.

- **Create Daily To-Dos**

   Make a list of small tasks that chip away at your milestones. These tasks should fit seamlessly into your day-to-day schedule.

- **Track Your Progress**

   Mark these tasks off as you complete them. Enjoyable apps like habit trackers can be particularly useful here.

- **Reward Yourself**

   Decide on small, meaningful rewards for completing each milestone. It helps reinforce positive behavior.

Look at the consistency like tending a plant. You **water** it regularly, giving it sunlight and the right nutrients – skip this, and it wilts. Reminding yourself why you started can also reignite that fire when it sputters. You may surprise yourself by how motivated you feel just by revisiting your initial reasons.

I read somewhere:

"Success is the sum of small efforts repeated day in and day out."

Simple words, yet powerful. **Staying disciplined doesn't mean staying strict twenty-four seven**; it means showing up, inch by inch, step by step, making it easier over time. And you're not alone in this. Others have walked a similar path. Seeking out and sharing your progress with a supportive community can lend additional courage and keep you accountable.

So, keep your eye on the prize, track every small step, reward yourself along the way, and you'll find that sustaining motivation isn't really that tricky. You're just feeding the fire, bit by bit.

Embracing Continuous Improvement (Kaizen)

Achieving lasting results won't occur from one monumental stride but from the steady drip of small drops—those seemingly minor, incremental changes add up over time.

Taking the principle of Kaizen to heart, let's make change enjoyable and workable, without feeling like we're moving mountains. Imagine aiming to read more. Instead of diving into that thick novel, begin with a couple of pages a day—as reading grows familiar, meatier chunks will soon feel effortless.

Now, maintaining a growth mindset is pivotal. Mistakes? Think of them as tickets to learning. Okay, didn't finish your book this month? No sweat—did you learn new words? Develop a habit of curiosity? Those are wins too! Positive self-discipline emanates from embracing these 'learning opportunities' rather than seeing setbacks as stumbling blocks.

Revisiting goals regularly is just as important... seriously, take time to breathe every now and then, look at where you are, what you're doing, and how things are going. Directions may shift and gather surprises; what worked once might not fit tightly anymore. Find comfort in knowing it's perfectly fine—better even—to adjust.

Here's a way to rethink strategy easily:

- **Set Your Core Goal**

  What's the big picture? Whether it's better health, honing a skill, or being more organized, choose your area of focus.

- **Break Down That Goal**

  What small steps get you there? For better health, it might be drinking more water, taking short walks, or swapping sweet snacks for fruits.

- **Start Tiny**

  Make those adjustments so easy they feel laughable at first. Drink a glass of water in the morning, take a 5-minute walk, grab an apple just once a day at the start.

- **Increase Gradually**

  As comfort goes up with your new habits, slowly expand your efforts. Those 5-minute walks may soon become 20-minute routines without fuss; the single fruit may branch out to varied healthy snacks throughout your day.

- **Monitor and Review**

  This step harbors the magic. Check back—is your walk routine becoming tedious? Try new paths. Increase effort only as you feel ready. Keep strategies flexible, mold them to fit.

Daily adjustments are real game-changers (Note: Not using "game-changer," but here it's apropos!), igniting a silent but steady wave driving you towards improvement. If today's strategy seems stale, tweak it—the goal isn't always to blow ahead fast but to chisel margins day by day. It's the project delightfully leaning towards betterment, inch by inch.

Let's have a block quote give your mind a little nudge:

"In small-corner shops, in world-wide conglomerates, in home workshops... where there's a hint of growth to bet on—it'll bloom when Kaizen wraps it up."

Implement these ideas practically in daily habits:

- For your career, apply incremental learning—adding new skills, one at a time.
- Dive into healthier habits, like incrementally choosing nutritious foods or slicing down sedentary time.
- Consider house organization; introduce small consecutive adjustments to your living space.
- Or tackle personal development by simply building in tiny segments of meditation or reflection.

No grandiose ceremony really needed. Winning results steep from sowing these daily tufts knowingly—welcoming the journey while nudging little efforts forward. Through diet, work, leisure, filing apps, maybe a quiet Sunday rearranging spaces (Marie Kondo anyone?)—find grander fulfillment post including these routines within.

Self-discipline thrives amidst this innovative whisper of Kaizen, like little bites even sweets can't surpass. Let's pivot, revel, check and rekindle disciplines earnestly.

No grand hoopla of seismic montages—but quietly, surely—changing one's universe gently **through** persistent improvement.

Balancing Rest and Effort for Longevity

Balancing rest and effort is like cooking a great meal—it requires careful timing and the right mix of ingredients. Do too much of one, and the whole thing falls apart. One of the tastiest "ingredients" is scheduling regular breaks. Say you've been working hard on an important project—hunched at your desk, deep in thought. Without a doubt, your brain and body need some **"breather moments."** It's not about taking time off but respecting the natural ebb and flow of your energy. I know it sounds counterintuitive, but breaks actually make you more productive. Every 90 minutes, stand up, stretch, get some air. Think of these as power pulses, recharging your batteries.

Next, consider this—a good night's sleep isn't a luxury; it's a necessity you can't ignore. I remember this one week where I shortchanged my sleep, trying to finish a big project. By the end, not only did my work suffer—I was cranky, made bad decisions, and had zero energy left for anything fun. Prioritize your sleep like you prioritize meetings: make it non-negotiable. Get those solid seven to eight hours; your body and mind will thank you. Your **"inner productivity machine"** runs better after regular sleep cycles, trust me.

And consider recovery, which is in the same league as sleep but often overlooked. Recovery means doing things that you enjoy and that make you feel good. Maybe it's a relaxed walk in the park (nature can reset a cluttered mind), a hobby like painting, or even sitting quietly with your favorite book. For instance, when I feel exhausted, dabbling in a bit of gardening almost always refreshes me. These aren't breaks but vital ingredients in the recipe for long-term energy.

We also need to talk about something many of us know all too well—burnout. It's kind of like cooking spaghetti at too high a heat; you just end up with a mess. Maintaining the delicate balance between "doing more" and "doing just enough" is essential. Approach your tasks with a sense of moderation. Burnout doesn't come overnight; it creeps up when you think pushing a bit more won't hurt. Kid yourself not. Sustainable effort means knowing your limits and listening to your body wicked attentively.

Step 1: Know when you're close to burnout

Active awareness is the secret here. Sense tension in your neck, eyes burning, feeling exceptionally sluggish? Take it as a signal to step back rather than pushing harder.

Step 2: Set boundaries with your work schedule

Stick to strict end times. If you work from 9 to 5, learn to shut off the computer at 5—even if that email isn't perfect.

Step 3: Refill, don't just rest

Recovery means engaging in activities that replenish your soul, whatever resonates with you. It's not about slouching on the couch with an episode of something. Intentionally get involved in relaxing activities.

Take breaks regularly, **prioritize sleep and recovery**, and **incorporate moderation in your tasks**—these are your evergreen tools for longevity.

When you're balanced, working towards goals feels less like a grind and more like an orchestration of sustained efforts.

"Take time to recharge and recover between your actions to achieve long-term success."

Balancing rest and effort, while appearing mundane, is the unsung hero of great accomplishments. Give your amazing self the gift of balance and see how far you'll go! And don't forget, the little steps like regular breaks, sleep, and enjoyable recovery are as important as the big goals you chase.

Integrating Self-Discipline into All Areas of Life

Applying **self-discipline** across different aspects of our lives is crucial if we want consistent progress. Imagine your personal, professional, and social spheres as parts of a pizza: each sector needs balance to taste just right.

In our personal lives, discipline could mean setting boundaries and establishing healthy routines. Think about waking up at the same time each day, even on weekends. I know it sounds tough, but trust me, those first few days will be hard...until it just becomes natural. Try setting small and achievable goals—drink a glass of water right after you wake up (you'll be surprised how much easier everything starts with that little push).

Professionally, discipline can transform our work from mere tasks to milestones of achievements. Develop a consistent work routine. That could translate into something like checking your emails only three times a day: morning, noon, and before you leave. Consistency allows your brain to 'switch on' when needed and take a break, creating effective mental waves for sharp performance.

Accountability is another big piece of the pie...and by pie, I mean life. In each aspect, keep yourself accurately accountable. For instance, in social settings, keeping promises made to friends and family helps maintain trust. Reflect on simple mistakes and own them – there's no shame in saying you forgot because you were too wrapped up in work. Make it right by planning better in the future.

Another important factor is expanding the application of these techniques. If you're punctual at work, why can't you show the same punctuality for hanging out with friends? If you plan meticulously for project deadlines, extend that skill to planning a holiday with loved ones. Blending these behaviours across various spheres links your disciplined habits together, creating one harmonious loop.

Let's make this practical. Starting with basic routines often works wonders. Simple morning routines are great examples:

- **Establish Wake-Up Time**

Set your alarm, and stick with it. Over time, your body clock will likely adapt to this consistency—making those mornings easier.

- **Morning Hydration**

Create a habit of drinking water first. Set a glass by your bed to remind you.

- **Quick Physical Activity**

Whether it's a 5-minute stretch or a short walk, getting your body in motion boosts both energy and mood for the day ahead.

Think about carrying these routines to work. Stick to a start hour just like your wake-up time. Have a "hydration break" scheduled (don't just reach for coffee by reflex). An afternoon stroll can mimic this quick physical break, giving your mind time to breathe.

Socially, consistency counts, too. Meeting friends for monthly brunches or weekly calls fortifies relationships because everyone appreciates reliability. If you assure your friend, "will call every Thursday"—make an event of it. Imagine mutually knowing you just gave each other a piece of well-planned time!

In everything you do, these disciplines sum up to a rhythmic, balanced life. Double-check if you skipped a weekly call, understand why it happened, and reschedule immediately rather than missing out entirely.

Consistency is not perfection, but a commitment applied in generality - letting it wane occasionally won't diminish its power; it only loses value when dismissed frequently.

Practical tips mesh so well into life that, over time, they become automated, conducting without constantly tapping on consciousness. Discipline doesn't have to be restrictive—it can present freedom through structured functioning.

So please start easy. One routine at a time, one instant accountability figured in, and extend these comfortably to enrich all aspects of your vibrant and interconnected life.

Now, excuse me while I set my alarm for tomorrow morning...

Reflection and Future Planning

We're here in the thick of it, reflecting on where we've come and dreaming about where we hope to go. Here's a key: regularly checking in with yourself is crucial. Just as athletes review their game tapes, we need to size up our strengths and weaknesses. The strong points give you confidence; the weak ones? They're action items.

Picture your day: when did you kill it, and when did things turn south? Identifying these pockets lets you gauge your performance realistically. Think of those times when you hit deadlines effortlessly (that's your strength, right?); now contrast them with times you didn't. Why did that happen? Did you struggle to get started?

Even more than acknowledging our strengths and weaknesses, it's super important to use this analysis to set future goals. For instance, if you can crank out impressive work without missing deadlines, you know you've got time management down. Make time for more challenging projects, diving deeper into complex stuff. It's the weak areas that call for deliberate, actionable plans.

"Often, success starts by deciding the specific challenges to take on."

The next piece of the puzzle is carving out growable pathways— actionable plans for continuous progress. We all have moments where we get sidetracked so, keeping everything actionable is vital. Ask yourself: what's the next small step? Then, take it. Consistency isn't built on major leaps but in the small, stacked steps. Transform simple actions into routine habits, like reviewing what went well every Friday afternoon.

Let me share a story: I remember meeting a friend who wanted to switch careers—a gigantic shift that seemed overwhelming. Together, we mapped out an actionable plan; she tackled small, manageable tasks every week and didn't lose sight of her goal. Fast forward to eight months later, she walked confidently into her new job industry, a shining example of planned effort paying off.

So, where do we even start?

- Make time to review:

  Life is so full of distractions; carve out specific periods just for reflection. A Sunday evening with a notepad could be your best tool here.

- Keep a balance sheet of strengths and weaknesses:

  A simple approach could change your life. Note what went great and what didn't and why that was.

(Note to self—being honest here isn't always easy, but it's non-negotiable.)

- Revisit past goals:

   This provides two massive benefits: you'll celebrate progress and understand why some goals weren't achieved.

Thinking ahead, daydreaming about what's next is exciting—and essential. This reflection should spark new, genuine, attainable goals. Was write a novel one of your priorities? Channel that introspective self, analyze why it didn't happen before, and factor in new tactics: allocate daily writing time, try writing apps, join a writers' group.

By mapping out these strategies, thinking about what's past can become proactive planning for the **brilliant** future.

Here's a crisp gameplan for perfecting it all:

Step 1: Self-Analysis

Be regularly dipping into strengths and weaknesses—yes, it's beneficial. This isn't about being harsh; it's about clarity.

Step 2: Set Goals from Past Insights

Make those strengths your launching pad for lofty, ambitious goals while concurrently addressing weaknesses (growth areas).

Step 3: Plan Your Pathway

Actionable plans—one small step after another. Define specific, easy daily or weekly steps that find and use your time effectively.

Fostering a **profound** habit of reflection not only helps in setting goals but enriches your life choices and the pathways to those sparkling dreams. Whether it's about minor triumphs or monumental shifts, reflection and future planning aren't just tasks—they're tools for crafting a path paved with the potential of even more success and fulfillment in life.

So, here's to joyful and honest reflection... and calculated plans for what's coming next.

Engage wholeheartedly and watch as magic happens!

Let's Get Practical!

Alright, let's **dive** straight into achieving lasting results through **discipline** — a crucial chapter that'll transform how you persevere and succeed over the long haul. This exercise will guide you, step by step, through sustaining **motivation**, keeping up the **momentum**, balancing efforts, and integrating **discipline** into all corners of your life. Let's get to work!

Step One: Clarify Your Long-Term Goals

Grab a notepad and jot down your major long-term goals. To make this practical, let's say you want to get fit, excel in your career, and develop a new hobby. Seeing these destinations black and white gives you a clear sense of where you're heading. Think of these goals as your north star — they guide every decision you make from here on out.

What to think: "I'm setting these goals not just for today, but for the legacy I want to create."

What to say: "I'm committed to running a marathon in a year, getting promoted in my job, and learning to play the guitar."

What to do: Write these down in big, bold letters and stick them somewhere you'll see them every day — maybe on your bathroom mirror or your fridge. Seeing them constantly keeps them fresh in your mind.

Step Two: Break Your Goals into Manageable Chunks

Big goals can be daunting, so break them down. Let's stick to our examples. Running a marathon becomes a plan to run 5k in a month,

10k in three months, and so on. Career-wise, aim to finish a key project this quarter. For guitar, maybe it's learning three chords this month.

What to think: "What small steps can I take today that'll get me closer to my big goals?"

What to say: "By the end mile run this month, create an awesome progress report, and play three simple songs by the end of summer."

What to do: Map these out in a planner or app, plotting exactly when you'll tackle each mini-goal.

Step Three: Stay Motivated Over Time

To keep up the drive, regularly remind yourself why you started. **Motivation** wavers, so find little rituals to reignite your fire. For instance, reward yourself with a delicious, healthy treat after each run or celebrate work victories with a fun outing.

What to think: "Remember the thrill reasons why this goal matters to me."

What to say: "I'm doing this to feel healthier, advance my career, and enrich my life with music."

What to do: Keep a "Motivation Journal" where you jot down personal victories, reasons for continuing, and positive feedback from others.

Step Four: Focus on Continuous Improvement

Adopt the Kaizen approach of small, continuous improvements. With fitness, this might mean tweaking your diet bit by bit. At work, allocate 10 minutes each day to research trends. For guitar, find little ways to get faster at chord changes.

What to think: "What tiny tweak can I make today that'll improve my progress a notch?"

What to say: "I'm going to add an extra vegetable to my meals, update one piece of knowledge for my job daily, and practice switching from G to C chords faster."

What to do: Set a reminder on your phone to make a tiny improvement each day. Celebrate these small steps; they cumulatively lead to big results.

Step Five: Balance Between Effort and Rest

Burnout is real. Schedule both work and relaxation into your daily routine. Say you exercise five days a week, with two rest days. In your career, ensure you have moments to unwind. The same should go for your guitar practice.

What to think: "Sustainability relies on balancing push and pause."

What to say: "I am dedicated to running only five days a week and enjoying guilt-free rest days, planning productive workhours as well as downtime, and practicing the guitar without overexerting."

What to do: Block out time slots in your calendar specifically for rest and relaxation. Use alarms or notifications to remind you when to pause.

Step Six: Integrate Discipline Into All Areas of Life

Start viewing **discipline** as a muscle — the more you exercise it in one area, the stronger it'll be in others. If you're disciplined about fitness, apply that same rigor to your financial habits. Routine strengthens over time and place.

What to think: "How can I use my **discipline** skills across different areas?"

What to say: "Using my exercise **discipline** model, I'll start budgeting and save a certain amount every month, and use specific learning times for continuous skill upgrading."

What to do: Write down and input these new habits into your daily routine. Mark regular appointments on your calendar to account for them.

Step Seven: Reflect and Plan Ahead

What gets measured, gets managed. Regularly review your progress and adjust your plans accordingly. After each month, examine how well you stuck to your exercise, work progress, or guitar practices. Evaluate, reflect, and iterate.

What to think: "How well did I stick to my plans this month and what small changes need to be made?"

What to say: "This month, I achieved my mini-goals X, Y, and Z. However, I found myself slipping a bit here and there. Here's how I can adjust to hit my targets even better."

What to do: Conduct a monthly review, write down what worked, what didn't, and tweak your plan for the next month accordingly.

By following these practical steps you're integrating different elements of **discipline** into cohesive daily habits. It's all about small, consistent actions leading to monumental results... let's keep pushing forward!

Conclusion

"As a man thinketh in his heart, so is he." This timeless phrase reminds us of the power of our inner thoughts and disciplines. We've come a long way since Chapter 1—understanding that positive self-discipline can be a transformative force in our lives.

Reflecting on **Part 1: Laying the Foundation**, the most valuable takeaway is that positive self-discipline isn't just a theory; it's deeply rooted in science and psychology. By understanding how our brains manage willpower and self-control, we gain insight into our behavioral patterns. The brain is a complex machine, with willpower operating like a muscle—strengthening through practice and positive emotions.

Part 2: Preparing for Success showcased practical tools and techniques to build robust structures in our daily lives. With goal-setting methodologies, habit formation strategies, and effective routines, we laid the groundwork for sustained success. Whether it was crafting SMART goals, using the WOOP method, or understanding the vital role of sleep and nutrition, each piece was a crucial step toward achieving personal growth and mental toughness.

In **Part 3: Practicing Positive Discipline**, the concepts came to life. The focus was on hands-on strategies like time management techniques, maintaining consistency, and celebrating small successes—all vital for lasting self-discipline. The importance of time management methods, such as the Pomodoro Technique and Time Blocking, can't be overstated—they directly contribute to maximizing our productivity and staying on course.

Now, let's summarize the essence of it all:

- **Positive self-discipline**: More than just controlling impulses; it's about channeling our energy positively.
- **Psychology of change**: Understanding our biases can help us conquer fears and build resilience.
- **Mental toughness**: Integral for executive functions, focus, and flexibility.
- **Goal setting and habits**: Foundational for success, aligned with a vision of growth.
- **Overcoming pitfalls**: Invaluable strategies against procrastination and unrealistic expectations.
- **Application in daily life**: Consistency and reflection play key roles in integrating these disciplines effortlessly.

So, what's the big takeaway? **Self-discipline isn't a struggle; it's an ally.** By approaching it positively and with an understanding mind, we're more likely to enhance our mental strength, achieve our goals, and enjoy better overall well-being.

Here's a call to action: **Apply these concepts daily.** Reflect on what inspires you from this book and start with one technique. Be compassionate with yourself—progress is a journey, not a sprint.

It's been a pleasure to walk through this exploration together. May the insights, ideas, and practical techniques stay with you—propelling you toward a future filled with achievement and personal growth. And always remember, every step forward, no matter how small, counts.

Farewell, and here's to your success!

A Review Would Help!

When you support an independent author, **you are supporting a dream**.

If you enjoyed the book, please consider leaving a review. Your honest feedback is incredibly valuable and can have a significant impact.

- **Click on the below link**
- **Select the cover of the book you purchased**
- **Click on Review**
- **Submit**

If you have suggestions for improvements, please send an email to the contacts provided at the link below. Alternatively, you can scan the QR code and follow the link once you select your book.

Your review only takes a few seconds to write but means the world in helping other readers discover this work. **Your voice matters.**

Visit this link to leave a feedback:

https://pxl.to/LoganMind

Join my Review Team!

Thank you for reading my book! Your support means the world to me. If you're an avid reader, I have an irresistible offer for you—get a free copy of my book in exchange for your honest feedback. Your insights would significantly help me improve future releases.

How to Join the ARC Team

- Click on the link or scan the QR code below.
- On the page that opens up, click on the book cover.
- Select "Join Review Team."
- Sign up to BookSprout.
- You'll receive notifications every time I release a new book!

Check out the extras here:

https://pxl.to/LoganMind

www.ingramcontent.com/pod-product-compliance
Lightning Source LLC
Chambersburg PA
CBHW051737020426
42333CB00014B/1350